FAMOUS *Folk from* BELFAST

Jane E M Crosbie

BALLYHAY BOOKS

First published by Ballyhay Books,
an imprint of Laurel Cottage Ltd.
Ballyhay, Donaghadee, N. Ireland 2019.
Copyrights Reserved.
© Text Jane E M Crosbie.
All rights reserved.
No part of this book may be reproduced or stored on any media
without the express written permission of the publishers.
Design & origination in N. Ireland.
Printed & bound by Bell & Bain Limited, Scotland
ISBN 978 1910657 13 3

Contents

Introduction   5

Famous Folk from Belfast

  Isabella Tod   7

  James Joseph Magennis VC   18

  William Thomson, Lord Kelvin   33

  Chaim Herzog   45

  Jack Kyle O.B.E.   60

  John Stewart Bell   73

  Henry Joy and Mary Ann McCracken   81

  James Ellis   97

  William and Margaret Pirrie   109

  Winnifred Carney   118

  Ruby Murray   131

  Sir Crawford McCullagh   137

  No Mean City:

    Men and Women who Built Belfast   161

Belfast and its Forgotten History   167

INTRODUCTION

For those of you who have read my earlier book, *Famous Folk from Co. Down*, you will know that my inspiration to take to the keyboard again after a hiatus of 22 years was the discovery that Sir Hans Sloane, from Killyleagh, invented milk chocolate. This discovery led to the question of how many other famous people came from my home county: the answer being, considerably more than were included in the final tome.

The inspiration for this book was just one woman. Isabella Tod.

I first encountered the redoubtable Miss Tod when I was a boarder at Victoria College where her portrait was displayed in the drawing room and I learnt that anyone who has even a passing knowledge of the history of women's suffrage and/or education in Ireland should know both her name and that of her greatest friend and cohort, Margaret Byers. Try as I might to include her in my Co. Down book, I was unable to find any concrete evidence that she spent any significant period of time in the County, and so I started to drop heavy hints to my publisher that another book was required, this time on Belfast, so that I could share the knowledge of this wonderful woman with a wider audience.

Once he agreed my immediate problem was who should I choose to accompany Isabella? As I have a great affection for the people and history of my adopted city and it has always intrigued me how a small town in shadow of the great Cave Hill played such a pivotal role in the history of not only our own island but also throughout the world my difficulty was not who to include but who I could bring myself to leave out.

There are many who I wanted to include, such as Frank Carson, Gerry Fitt, Louis MacNeice, William Conor, or the serial killer Dr John Bodkin Adams, but pressures of space precluded them.

Famous Folk from Belfast

To arrive at my final selection, I have tried pick individuals whose stories demonstrate the variety of life in Belfast over the centuries. From the radicals of the late seventeenth century to the men and women who helped to shape the twentieth, sometimes at a local level, sometimes on a world stage.

The history of Belfast can be very frustrating and infuriating at times, as it has been one where events and the memory of them were often driven by sectarian divisions. As such there are parts of our history that we have forgotten to remember, because they don't fit the narrative of these divisions. I am sure that there will be some who will think for example that I have included too many Presbyterians, but the fact is that the men and women who built and developed Belfast, especially from around 1750-1850, were predominantly Presbyterian and in many cases, the McCrackens and Joys for example, it was their Presbyterian faith that informed and drove their actions. On a purely personal level I would have liked to include more women but, in a further example of selective memory, all too often the surviving information is too scant to show the contribution they undoubtedly made.

This is obviously not a definitive history of Belfast. If you are interested to find out more about that, then may I suggest the books by W A Maguire and Jonathan Bardon, both of which are excellent. Having said that, I do hope that you enjoy this book and the light it shines on some of this city's finest daughters and sons. I am now going to have to go and do some housework, having been able to avoid it for the past few months!

Jane E M Crosbie

ISABELLA TOD
1836-1896

Feminist, Suffragist, Political and Social Reformer

Isabella was perhaps Ireland's greatest and most successful campaigner to improve women's rights. She pursued this goal on all fronts from education to voting rights and from property rights to repeal of the Contagious Diseases Acts. Her success greatly improved to lot of women throughout Ireland.

I am not sure whether I should admit this or not but there are times when I think about an individual and a 'theme-song' plays in my mind. Not all the time, of course, but just for some significant individuals. One such individual is Isabella Tod and the tune, or rather in her case snippet, that plays are the words from *Land of Hope and Glory*. Every time I think about her the words *how shall we extol thee, who are born of thee* are playing in the background. For 50% of the population in the late nineteenth century, she was a physical embodiment of a land of hope and glory. That women in Ireland live the lives they do, with the privilege of full enfranchisement, with autonomy over their own bodies and property, with access to full education is thanks to the efforts of Isabella Tod and those who followed her. They fought to improve the lives of women, of every social strata, of every religion. This does not just apply to women in Ireland, but also in England, Scotland and Wales.

Famous Folk from Belfast

And yet, ask most people about her and you will be met with a blank stare. They will have heard about the Pankhursts, they may even have heard about Millicent Fawcett, but Isabella Tod?

So who was she and why was she so important?

Maria Luddy in *Women, Power and Consciousness in nineteenth century Ireland* states that:

> 'To write the life of Isabella Maria Susan Tod is to write a history of feminist activity in Ireland from the 1860s to the time of her death in 1896. Tod was the outstanding advocate of women's rights during this period.'

Not a lot is known about Isabella's early life. She was born in Edinburgh in 1836 to James Banks Tod, a merchant, and Maria Isabella Waddell from a well-known Presbyterian family. We know that she had at least one brother, Henry, and a niece, Mrs. Groffier, both of whom lived in London. When her father died in the 1850s Mrs. Tod and Isabella moved to Belfast and joined the Elmwood Presbyterian congregation. Isabella's mother, of whom nothing is known other than her name, was the guiding light in Isabella's life. In fact she often said, *"I always feel I am my mother's mouthpiece."* Isabella had been educated at home by her mother who as well as encouraging her to read as widely as possible also made sure that she was aware of her family's history. Isabella's maternal uncle, Rev Hope Masterton Waddell was one of the first Irish Presbyterian missionaries to the Caribbean and her maternal great-grandfather was Rev. Charles Masterton, minister of Rosemary Street Presbyterian, a colonel in the Belfast Irish Volunteers in the 1780s[1]. She was proud of her radical heritage and often stated that she *"came of fighting stock"*.

---

1. The Rosemary Street congregation was very active in radical politics in the late eighteenth century. Several of the founders of the United Irishmen were members of the congregation.

Isabella Tod

Isabella's Presbyterian faith was very important in shaping the rest of her life, indeed it informed and motivated every aspect of who she was.

Presbyterians are often painted as dour and judgmental, but throughout history they have often been radical thinkers and activists as true Presbyterianism promotes and encourages freedom of thought and there is a great emphasis on the importance of education. One American website[2] notes that:

> 'In times past when Presbyterians arrived in a new place, they would usually build a church, a school, and a hospital, in that order. Presbyterians see the right to worship of God as paramount, and education as necessary, so that they can serve the world in God's name'.

Isabella was a full member of the Church and as such had the right to vote within the it. In the Presbyterian Church votes of the laity and the clergy have equal value [as ministers are merely teaching elders[and Isabella was convinced that if she was able to vote to elect her minister and elders then she should also be able to vote for her council representative or M.P. As she said herself:

> 'It is impossible for women to do their duty, and to protect their interests and dignity without the same weapon men find essential for the same'.[3]

In the 1860s Belfast was the largest and wealthiest port in Ireland. The population of around 100,000 was being augmented every year as people left the land and flooded into the town to seek work. The dismal living conditions that had led to the rapid spread of disease during the Famine years, were slowly improving but many, if not most of the workers lived in slum conditions that we would

---

2. *https://www.newsmax.com/fastfeatures/presbyterians-protestant-beliefs-christians/2015/04/02/id/635819/*

3. Tod, Women and the New Franchise Bill

find hard to comprehend today. As a member of the newly formed Elwood Presbyterian congregation, she undertook charitable work amongst the poor in Belfast and what she witnessed drove her to campaign to change society for the better, especially for women.

Isabella began to write for newspapers such as the *Northern Whig* and the *Banner of Ulster*[4] on a range of social issues, especially concerning the living conditions of the poor and education for women. By 1867 she had become sufficiently well known to be invited to present a paper to the AGM of the National Association for the Promotion of Social Science, held that year in Belfast. Her paper, *On advanced education for girls of the upper and middle classes,* was actually presented by a man but this was the last time that she would allow a man to talk for her.

Through her charity work, Tod had met and become friends with Margaret Byers[5], the founder of what became Victoria College[6]. Together they formed a formidable and unstoppable team in the campaign to promote and improve the education available to women and girls. There is not really enough room in this chapter to discuss all their achievements in this sphere, but there are two which will give a flavour of their determination to raise female education to full academic degrees.

---

4. *Banner of Ulster* was a Presbyterian newspaper established in 1842 by Rev. William Gibson, the minister of the Rosemary Street Presbyterian congregation. It was published on Tuesday and Friday but when the other Belfast Newspapers began daily publication its readership declined and it ceased publication in 1870.

5. Margaret Byers was the leading educationalist sine qua non in nineteenth century Ireland. Amongst her other major achievements, her insistence that all teachers [from kindergarten upwards] had a formal qualification in their subject raised the standard of education not only for her 'young ladies' but also for all schoolchildren in Belfast and further afield. See Famous folk from Co. Down by myself or Alison Jordan's biography Margaret Byers: pioneer of women's education and founder of Victoria College Belfast.

6. Originally called the Ladies Collegiate School, Byers opened her school in Wellington Place [1859] with 35 pupils. Such was her success that it moved to larger premises in Howard Street, and then Pakenham Place, before moving into purpose built premises at Lower Crescent in 1874. The Crescent Arts Centre now uses the building.

Isabella Tod

Alison Jordan, in her excellent biography of Mrs. Byers, states that:

> 'There was a great deal of wool-work parrots and roses in mid-nineteenth century women's education, and knowledge of arithmetic and English grammar was meager indeed.'

Indeed arguments were put forward by respected academics of the day that higher education would damage women's health and/or women were being impertinent to wish for degrees. Both Tod and Byers were dismissive of these arguments. Tod argued that:

> 'a wise and wide course of education not only teaches much absolutely, but, what is of far more importance, so enlarges and strengthens the mind, so instructs it how to learn, as to prepare it for all the contingencies of life.'

Further she argued that:

> 'self-improvement is the first law of civilized nature, and we have no notion of disobeying it.'

Both women fought for and won the right for female pupils to take their degree examinations through the Royal University of Ireland. Until the hallowed portals of the Irish University Colleges were finally opened to both sexes in 1890, women graduates received their tuition and took their examinations through affiliated colleges, of which Victoria College was one. By 1874, only 4 years after the examinations were opened up to women 13 candidates from Victoria College had won Honours certificates[7]. In 1878 she and Mrs. Byers successfully lobbied in the heart of government at Westminster to have girls included in the new Intermediate Education (Ireland) Act, which provided for standardized examinations throughout all ages of school children. In later life Isabella

---

7. Not only did Victoria College graduates top the list of women's colleges each academic year, but also Victoria College Belfast came third overall after University College Dublin and University College Belfast.

said that *'One thing I am very proud of ... is getting girls included in the Intermediate Education Act of 1878.'* They had travelled to Westminster with the local MP, J P Corry, and directly lobbied, amongst others, the Lord Chancellor, Lord Cairns, and James Lowther, Chief Secretary for Ireland.

Through her charitable work amongst the poorest families in Belfast, Isabella had seen at first hand how a dependence or abuse of alcohol coupled with the lack of female property rights could not only damage but also irreparably destroy the lives of the most vulnerable in society. There was an Irish Temperance League already in existence but together with Mrs. Byers, Tod was dissatisfied by the male domination of this organisation and so, in 1874, they formed the Belfast Women's Temperance Association. They recognised the face that women suffered most from the 'evils of intemperance.' While they advocated total abstinence they were not convinced that formal legislation was required. Instead they hoped to lead by example and the following year they opened three 'refreshment houses' one of which also offered 'nutritious dinner to girls engaged in factories'. They also established a Prison Gate Mission, an home for inebriate women, gave classes in cookery and hygiene, and opened a home for destitute girls which offered a basic education as well as instruction in skills that would prepare them for the work-place.

Such was Tod's influence that in 1868, a mere year after her first public paper, she was the only woman called to give evidence to the Select Committee inquiry on the Married Women's Property Bill[8]. Using the information she had acquired through her charity work, in addition to person observations among her own, middle-class, circle of family and friends, the evidence she gave was stark and compelling. She argued that working class women should be

---
8. Tuesday, 14 July 1868.

Isabella Tod

able to retain control over their own income. When asked what effect the status quo had upon the men themselves she answered:

> "*It certainly makes them more careless of their responsibility to support their family. It also encourages them in dissipate habits, knowing as they do that they have some resource to fall back on.*"

Nor was she only concerned with the working class women. She told of one lady of her acquaintance who was left destitute due to the 'dissipated habits' of her husband, despite having had a sizeable inheritance from a relative.[9] Tod had helped to found a branch of the Married Women's Property Committee in Belfast and later served on the executive of the national committee, which brought her into contact with fellow campaigners such as Elizabeth Wolstenholme and Josephine Butler.

Through her friendship with Josephine Butler, Isabella became a vocal advocate and campaigner for the repeal of the Contagious Diseases Acts of which there were three in 1864, 1866 and 1869. The acts were introduced as the authorities were very concerned by the rampant spread of sexually transmitted diseases among every stratum of society, but especially among the military and navy. Their solution was to control the women who had the disease, leaving the men free to continue to spread it among the sex workers and their own wives. One of the most contentious provisions within the acts was that any woman who was suspected of being a prostitute, especially in naval and garrison towns, could be arrested and subjected to an internal examination. Should she be found to be suffering from a STD she was then allowed to be incarcerated in either a Lock Ward (clue in the name) or in a workhouse infirmary and subjected to a variety of supposed cures. The first National Association for the Repeal of the Contagious

---

9. The relative, who lived overseas, had been unable to find local Trustees to try to protect the inheritance from the husband. The use of Trustees to protect 'family' money from dissolute husbands continued well into the twentieth century.

Diseases Act was formed in 1869, but barred women from taking part in, or even attending, any of their meetings. Outraged by this a group of women including Josephine Butler, Isabella Tod and a former nurse called Florence Nightingale, formed their own Ladies NARCDA. Between 1870 and 1885 Isabella tirelessly toured the island of Ireland speaking to groups of women from every strata of society, collecting signatures for several of the 17,365 petitions presented to Parliament by both Associations. The acts were eventually repealed in 1886.

One of the tragedies of the story of Isabella's life is the fact that while she saw great success in many of her campaigns, the one that was closest to her heart did not succeed within her own lifetime – women's suffrage.

Everything that she achieved was through the use of political power, but she was restricted from exercising that power through the ballot box, not because of her religion, her class or even her lack of formal education but simply because of her sex. As she campaigned to improve the lives of women of all classes, but especially the least in society, her own political impotence gained a greater significance. She was by no means the first or the only woman to rail against the disenfranchisement of half of the population, but in Ireland she was certainly one of the most vocal and most important.

For Isabella the vote was essential to promote God's work within society. In an article entitled: *The New Crusade and Women's Suffrage* she argued that it was:

> '... *not only for the help which women must give to women, but even more, for the discharge of their special duty to the whole state – a duty which God has entrusted to them, and which no man can do – women are bound to demand their immediate admission within the electorate.*'

Isabella Tod

In 1871 she established the North of Ireland Women's Suffrage Committee, the first such society in Ireland and campaigned tirelessly to have women admitted to the franchise on the same terms as men.[10] She was to have limited success within her own lifetime, most importantly in 1887 when the Belfast Corporation decided to extend the franchise to all ratepayers. She lobbied extensively and got the wording in the bill changed from 'man' to 'person'. Just in case anyone tried to worm their way out of it she also succeeded in getting the definition of the word person as being a man or a woman inserted. This meant that the women of Belfast were the first women in Ireland to be able to vote in municipal elections. In a letter to the *Northern Whig* following the passing of the bill Isabella expressed the hope:

> *'that the newly enfranchised women voters will care less for "merely party politics" than less enlightened men do, and that they will care more for the great social and moral questions of the day.'*

There is a clue in this last quote as to why Isabella is largely forgotten today. She lost many friends in both Ireland and the rest of the UK through her opposition to the Home Rule Bill. Isabella had many friends within the Liberal party, up to and including Gladstone himself, but she was horrified by the prospect of Home Rule. Her opposition had nothing to do with sectarianism; in fact it was based on just the opposite. She was convinced that the only way in which the island of Ireland could develop non-sectarian politics, as well as continuing to flourish economically, was within the political union. In the *Northern Whig* on 14 April 1886 she wrote that:

---

10. The 1884 Representation of the People Act had extended the vote to all men over the age of 21 who either paid an annual rent of £10 or held property to land valued at more than £10.

Famous Folk from Belfast

> '*they suppose that this opposition arises from religious bigotry and need to have it brought strongly before them that what we dread is the complete dislocation of all society ... and to organized freedom of action ... it is needful to point out that the conditions of a free democracy do not exist in Ireland. Before they can exist the two great training influences of widespread education and large local government must have room to be fairly brought into operation.*'

Again in 1892 she wrote of her horror of proposed Home Rule:

> '*Knowing Ireland thoroughly ... I shrank in horror from the revival of the religious and racial difference which was certain to ensue.*'

It was not that she thought that Ireland was unable to govern herself, she was convinced that for 'free democracy', by which she meant 'normal' politics based on ideological and social concerns to flourish and for the sectarianism that then as now dominated political debate to decline, Ireland was better off as a full and equal partner within the United Kingdom and economically was better off as part of the Empire. To put it in more topical terms she was a remainer.

True to form she formed a Liberal Women's Unionist Association in Belfast which presented a petition signed by 30,000 women throughout the island, which was presented to Queen Victoria asking her to withhold royal assent should the bill be passed. It through her involvement in the LWUA she became friends with Millicent Garrett Fawcett and spoke on platforms with her throughout England. Maria Luddy argues that:

> '*her fight to oppose the various Home Rule Bills placed her on a par with many male politicians of the period.*'

During her final decade, while she continued to travel throughout Ireland, England, Scotland and Wales promoting her main interests of suffrage, education and temperance as well as taking up new causes, she struggled against ill-health. In fact her last public ap-

Isabella Tod

pearance, days before her death, was on the platform at a meeting of behalf of distressed Armenians. She died at home on 8 December 1896 attended by Dr Byers, the son of her friend Margaret. When news of her death was announced obituaries appeared in every major newspaper throughout the United Kingdom including the *Irish Times, London Illustrated Times,* and *London Evening Standard.*

So why was Tod forgotten about? Luddy argues that:

> '*the fact that she was a woman clearly played some role in her disappearance from Irish history. Perhaps too the fact that she was a Unionist has made her less appealing to historians writing on Irish history.*'

But I would dispute the certainty of the last part, [see chapter on Winifred Carney]; instead I would argue that it was the fact that she was a woman. I was only aware of her because I was awarded the Isabella Tod scholarship[11] while at school, and because she was a friend of Mrs. Byers. It is still possible to read very well researched books on the history of Belfast in the nineteenth century that barely mention the campaign for women's suffrage, much less name the driving light in the movement.

Isabella Tod is buried in the Balmoral Cemetery. Her epitaph says it all.

Many daughters hath done virtuously but thou excellest them all.

---

11. Worth a massive £15 – the amount had not increased since it was first awarded shortly after her death.

JAMES JOSEPH MAGENNIS VC
1919-1986
Mini-submariner, diver

James Magennis's bravery during a midget submarine attack on Japanese warships in Singapore during the last days of the war saw him become the only person from N. Ireland to be awarded the Victoria Cross during WWII.

The only person from Northern Ireland to be awarded the Victoria Cross during the Second World War, James was born in Belfast on 29 October 1919 the second son and middle child of William and Mary McGinnes of Majorca Street, just off the Grosvenor Road. He had two brothers, William and Anthony, and two sisters Rosemary and Peggy. Family legend had it that the midwife dropped him into a basin of water and so his future career below the sea was set at birth. While he was still in the infant department at St Finian's school, his father returned to his native Scotland in search of work and was never heard from again. Mary was left with five small children to rear on the limited wages she could get from part-time work and one family friend told Magennis's biographer, George Fleming, that:

> 'Mrs McGinnes at one time had to put four of her children into temporary care in Nazareth House orphanage on the Ormeau Road.'

James Magennis

It was while at school that James learnt how to swim at the Falls Road Swimming Baths. His friends remember that he would spend as much time as he possibly could in the water.

James left school at 14 and started work in a wine store. He then got a job selling ice cream in a fish and chip shop, but his tendency to 'treat' his friends resulted in him being sacked, as he himself recounted, *'for being too generous'*. Jobs for unskilled workers in 1930s Belfast were few and far between, and almost non-existent for teenage boys. James's older brother William had joined the Royal Navy a few years earlier and so it was not a surprise when James enlisted in the Royal Navy in 1935 as a boy seaman. He later told a newspaper reporter:

> *'I wanted to be a soldier but the army turned me down. 'Your education is not good enough,' said the Belfast recruiting officer. So I joined the navy. I was just fifteen, a pale faced city lad when I was introduced to the tough life of HMS GANGES, the boy's training establishment at Shortly, Suffolk'.*

It was at this time that the spelling of his name was changed when due to an administrative error he was enlisted as James Magennis rather than McGinnes. By the time the mistake was discovered it seemed like too much hard work to get it altered and so he remained as Magennis throughout his naval career. He was sent initially for basic training along with two other boys from Belfast and the tough regime came as a shock to most recruits. While flogging had been abandoned, caning or 'cuts' had not, although James never misbehaved sufficiently to warrant such a punishment. According to Fleming:

> *'Jim's upbringing in West Belfast, and just as tough De la Salle Brothers schooling, gave him a good grounding for the time he spent at GANGES'*

Famous Folk from Belfast

In later life he was to remember his time there and the life-long friendships he forged with the other ratings with a degree of affection.

On 6 March 1936, James started his first posting as a First Class Boy Seaman on board *HMS ROYAL SOVEREIGN* and set to sea the next day.

On the 6 March 1936 set sail onboard *HMS ROYAL SOVEREIGN* to rendezvous with his first ship *HMS DAUNTLESS* at Gibraltar, prior to sailing to India. A few months later he was transferred to *HMS ENTERPRISE* on patrol in the Indian Ocean. He was promoted to Ordinary Seaman, with a rise in pay to 26 shillings a week, in October 1937. In May 1938 he was transferred, yet again, to *HMS HERMES*, an aircraft carrier, and gained promotion to Able Seaman in October of that year. At the beginning of August 1939 he was transferred to *HMS DEFIANCE* in Devonport, for a torpedo course, and it was while he was here that war was declared on Germany on 1 September 1939.

In October 1939 he was drafted to *HMS KANDAHAR*, a 36-knot destroyer that was part of Lord Louis Mountbatten's fifth flotilla, and at last qualified for his daily 'tot' of rum, when he celebrated his 20th birthday later in the month.

It was while serving onboard *KANDAHAR*, on the 9th and 10th May 1940, that James took part in one of the most publicised naval incidents of the war[1].

While hunting U-boats in the North Sea, *KANDAHAR* was sailing with Lord Louis's *HMS KELLY* when *KELLY* was hit by a torpedo, which smashed into the forward boiler room, killing 27 officers and men and seriously wounding many more. *KANDAHAR* went

---

1. This was later made into a film starring Noel Coward as Lord Louis, In which we serve [1942]

James Magennis

to their aid and in the early morning James and the survivors took part in a short funeral service as the dead were buried at sea. Many years later, in 1969, he told the *Daily Mail* that:

> 'Fear came to me when the smoke of battle had died down; when all that lingered was a dawn mist that hung like funeral crepe ... It was the sight of the dead and dying that struck real fear in me for the first time of my life. It made me sick. It paralysed me'.

No sooner had *KANDAHAR* helped to escort *KELLY* back into port, then on 17 May she was ordered to join 3 other destroyers[2] in the Red Sea, to again hunt enemy submarines. It was here, between 23-25 June, that they captured and sank a number of Italian submarines, and James displayed great personal courage by diving into shark infested waters to help rescue Italian submariners from the submarine *TORRECELLI* and drag them to safety. A fellow crew mate, Ervine Fleming, later commented:

> "It would be honourable enough to do the same for one's own shipmates, but Mick was risking his neck for the enemy."[3]

In May 1941 *KANDAHAR* was back in the Mediterranean, taking part in the Battle of Crete. Together with *FIJI, GREYHOUND, GLOUCESTER, JUNO* and *KINGSTON*, they were tasked with preventing German reinforcements landing on the island of Crete. On the 22 May, *GREYHOUND* was sunk and James took part in the rescue mission, in charge of a Whaler [rowing launch] picking up survivors from the oil covered sea, while coming under sustained air attack with bombs and machine guns. Worse was to come when *FIJI* was damaged and had to be abandoned, and *JUNO* received a direct hit, was broken in half and sank within minutes. Fleming described James's bravery:

---

2. HMS KINGSTON, KHARTOUM and KIMBERLEY.
3. Throughout his career in the Royal Navy James was nicknamed Mick, by his friends and shipmates.

Famous Folk from Belfast

'Unbelievable is the only word I would use to describe Mick's actions. I saw him repeatedly risk his own life to dive into furnace fuel oil and burning diesel to bring other shipwrecked sailors out. I lost count of the times we had to fish him out, and in he would go again. His actions were even more remarkable considering he was in real danger of being left behind. Ships under attack had to speed away and manoeuvre constantly to avoid the Stukas ... dozens of sailors owed their lives to Magennis and others who jumped into treacherous waters to rescue them'.

In December 1941 he was serving on *HMS KANDAHAR* when it was mined off the coast of Libya, when sailing through a minefield to try to rescue survivors from *NEPTUNE*, which itself had hit a mine.[4] Badly damaged the order was given to abandon ship and the 8 officers and 170 ratings had to swim to *HMS JAGUAR* who had come to their rescue. The ship's crew were sent back to England and awarded two weeks 'survivors leave'. His arrival at the family home came as a great, but pleasant, shock for his mother who had been told that he was 'missing, presumed dead.' By this stage of the war, all three of Mrs McGinnis's sons were serving in the Royal Navy as the youngest, Anthony, had signed up as soon as he was old enough.

After his 'survivors' leave, James returned to the torpedo school *HMS DEFIANCE*. While there he was delighted to be told that he was going to be drafted to *HMS BELFAST*, which was going to visit his home town, but this was not to be as he and Bernard Warwick were 'volunteered' for submarine service instead. Any disappoint-

---

4. Of the 765 officers and men on board HMS NEPTUNE only Able Seaman Norman Walton survived. His is a harrowing tale. *'I swam to a raft some 40 yards away. By that time around 30 men had clambered in and around it. It was designed for four... Little did I realize I would be clinging to that raft for a total of 5 and a half days as my shipmates slowly died around me ... by first light there were only 16 of us left. By the fourth day only four of us were left ... By Christmas there were only 2 of us left, myself and a Leading Seaman. An Italian aircraft spotted us and an Italian destroyer picked us up.'* They were only 4 miles off the Libyan coast when they were hit.

ment he may have felt at the change of plans would have been offset by the extra pay that service onboard a submarine attracted.[5] The extra pay was official recognition for the danger that service below the waves attracted. The prime minister Winston Churchill said in 1941 that:

> '*There is no branch of his Majesty's Forces which in this war has suffered the same proportion of fatal loss as our submarine service. It is the most dangerous of all services.*'

As Fleming says:

> '*The submarine was an essential part of the World War II navy and the men who served on these craft therefore had to really know their job.*'

Following basic training the 'volunteers' were sent to *CYCLOPS* in Rothesay, Scotland to complete his training onboard one of the H class submarines. James was on board *H50* as it patrolled the Irish Sea between Scotland and the Northern Irish ports of Belfast, Larne and Londonderry. Accommodation was cramped with off duty men sleeping in a torpedo rack. James spent most of 1942 in submarine training and it was as he was approaching the end of his training that he heard about new, smaller submarines called X-craft and that the powers that be were looking for volunteers for special service. He volunteered and registered for special service on 15 March 1943. He later recalled that before selection he had to undergo psychological evaluation including questions such as 'What are your hobbies' and 'Do you like cats?' He obviously passed the evaluation [although I have not been able to discover if he did like cats] and reported to *HMS VARBELL* base in Scotland for extra training, including diving training. The diving courses were very intensive and many, then as now, were failed.

---

5. Between 9d to 3 shillings and 9d per day, depending on rank and type of job.

Famous Folk from Belfast

I think it is important to pause here to look at the X class of midget submarines. Whilst doing the research for this section I had read about how the XEs were 53.25 feet long and 5.75 feet wide which, to be honest, really didn't mean much. However I came across a short Pathé News clip which featured one of these vessels[6] and it was immediately apparent how small they were and how incredibly cramped conditions must have been for the crew.

The midget subs were manned by 4 volunteers – usually a Lieutenant (in command), a Sub-Lieutenant, an Engine Room Artificer (usually Chief Petty Officer/Engineer who operated and maintained the machinery) and a Seaman or Leading Seaman. At least one of the crew would be a qualified diver.

The midget submarine's mode of attack was to be towed as close as possible to where their target was anchored [while remaining undiscovered] and then to make their own way to a position underneath the target. Once in position they could drop a mine [consisting of two tons of Amatol] under the target and the submarine's trained diver could attach limpet mines to the target's hull. If all went well the midget submarine could then retreat before the charges exploded.

Prior to the action in 1945 which led to his VC, James Magennis was mentioned in despatches for his actions during Operation Source, in September 1943, just 9 months after he had started his training as a mine warfare diver.[7]

The German army had invaded Norway in April 1940 and used the many coastal *fiords* to berth many of their warships and U-boats, ideally placed to attack the Arctic convoys, including the mighty warship *TIRPITZ*. Her better-known sister ship *BISMARCK* had

---

6. *https://www.britishpathe.com/video/midget-sub-to-cross-atlantic* which shows the size and conditions.

7. Operation Source was an action aimed at neutralizing the German fleet in Norway.

James Magennis

been sunk in 1941 but *TIRPITZ* remained to present a real and active danger to Allied ships. In September 1943 RAF reconnaissance reports said that *TIRPITZ* and two other ships were in Altenfjord and an attack was ordered.

All six X craft were to be used in the attack but first they had to get there. James was on board *X7* as it was towed behind the 'mother' submarine[8], on a six inch nylon cable 1000 miles across the North Sea. The voyage was dangerous with most of the X craft breaking their tow at some stage including *X9* which on 16 September broke its tow and was never seen again. The voyage took eight days. James didn't take part in the actual attack. Of the six X craft that had left Scotland four were left to launch the attack. *X6* and *X7* both managed to drop their charges under *TIRPITZ* but were spotted, attacked and had to be abandoned. Six of the eight submariners were captured but sadly the other two drowned. As a result of the mission *TIRPITZ* was badly damaged and remained out of action until April 1944. She was destroyed by an bombardment by the RAF in November 1944. Lt Donald Cameron *[X6]* and Lt Basil Place *[X7]* were both awarded the VC.

After Christmas leave in Bradford with his mother and sister Rosemary[9], James was transferred back to *BONAVENTURE* in Scotland to help train new officers for the new XE midget submarines and it was here that a chance encounter changed the course of his naval career. He later recalled:

> *'in 1944 one of [the] new officers was Lt. Ian Fraser… [h]e had new ideas. 'Magennis', he said one afternoon, 'you are a leading torpedo operator and know all about the electrics. It would be a good thing if I had a man aboard who could do another job beside diving.'*

---

8. Due to the arduous conditions on board one crew would man the submarine during along transit to be replaced by a fresh crew for the actual attack

9. James' sister Peggy had died in her teens and his remaining sister Rosemary and his mother had moved to England to work in the GEC aeroplane factory.

Famous Folk from Belfast

Within days he was on his way to Portsmouth for a special diving course and joined the XE craft operational crew. After 6 months training in early 1945 the six XE craft were loaded on to the *BONAVENTURE* to be transported, via the Caribbean to the Pacific theatre of war. It was during his first dive in the warmer waters of the Caribbean that he had his first encounter with sharks and told his brother Bill '*I saw some small sharks and later a barracuda while under, they both sniffed around me then lost interest, but I was honestly scared to death.*'

Operation Struggle, during which he was awarded his VC, took place in the last days of the war. With the benefit of hindsight it may now seem pointless, but it must be remembered that the Japanese may have been in retreat but they were in no way defeated and only a very few people on the entire planet knew that the Americans were about to drop atomic bombs on 6th and 9th August, which finally led to their surrender.

Thus on 31 July 1945, *HMS XE1* and *HMS XE3* executed a joint attack on two Japanese warships at anchor in Singapore harbour which threatened the advancing Allied forces. *XE1* was tasked with mining the heavy cruiser *MYŌKŌ* while *XE3's* target was the heavy cruiser *TAKAO*. Joining Magennis in *XE3* were Lieutenant Ian Edward Frazer, Royal Naval Reserve, Sub-Lieutenant William James Lanyon Smith, Royal New Zealand Naval Volunteer Reserve, and Engine Room Artificer 3rd Class Charles Alred Reed, Royal Navy.

Their approach to their target took 11 hours, at any time during which they could have been spotted by the enemy. To understand James's actions during the subsequent attack it is best to reproduce the citation for the VC that was published in the *London Gazette* on Tuesday, 13 November 1945.

James Magennis

Temporary Acting Leading Seaman James Magennis D/JX 144907.

Leading Seaman Magennis served as Diver in His Majesty's Midget Submarine *XE-3* for her attack on 31st July, 1945, on a Japanese cruiser of the Atago class. Owing to the fact that *XE-3* was tightly jammed under the target the diver's hatch could not be fully opened, and Magennis had to squeeze himself through the narrow space available.

He experienced great difficulty in placing his limpets on the bottom of the cruiser owing both to the foul state of the bottom and to the pronounced slope upon which the limpets would not hold. Before a limpet could be placed therefore Magennis had thoroughly to scrape the area clear of barnacles and in order to secure the limpets he had to tie them in pairs by a line passing under the cruiser keel. This was very tiring work for the diver, and he was moreover handicapped by a steady leakage of oxygen which was ascending in bubbles to the surface. A lesser man would have been content to place a few limpets and then return to the craft. Magennis, however, persisted until he had placed his full outfit before returning to the craft in an exhausted condition. Shortly after withdrawing, Lieutenant Fraser endeavoured to jettison his limpet carriers, but one of these would not release itself and fall clear of the craft. Despite his exhaustion, his oxygen leak and the fact that there was every probability of his being sighted, Magennis at once volunteered to leave the craft and free the carrier rather than allow a less experienced diver to undertake the job. After seven minutes of nerve-racking work he succeeded in releasing the carrier. Magennis displayed very great courage and devotion to duty and complete disregard for his own safety.

Although the attack had not sunk the *TAKAO* it had blown a 23 x 10ft hole in her hull and buckled her keel totally disabling the ship. Within days the war was over and the crew had returned to a naval base in Australia. It was here that James received notification on 13 November 1945, direct from Buckingham Palace, that he had been awarded the VC. He later remembered that:

> *I was proud but embarrassed. It was an ordeal for a matelot to be thrust into the limelight … There was just one whirl of parties, sherry, champagne, cocktail parties the lot. No-one expected me to work. I was excused everything … I took off to visit friends … when I returned two days later a policeman hurried up to me on the street.*

Famous Folk from Belfast

"The whole city has been searching for you. A plane is standing by to fly you home,: he said.

The flight back home stopped for a few hours in Singapore, where James and his fellow VC Lieutenant Ian Fraser were able to see the results of their actions during a visit to the harbour. Their arrival home to Poole, Dorset, was a bit of an anticlimax as there was no-one to meet them and they had to borrow their fare to London from the nearby naval base. When they both arrived in London they were invited to the BBC and then taken to the Phoenix Theatre to see a play. At the start of the interval the manager approached them to say that Queen Mary was in the Royal Box and wanted to meet them. James later recounted that she had said *You are Magennis, how do you do, young man? I feel deeply honoured to shake your hand.'* She chatted to them both for several minutes before saying *'Young man, I think my son will only be too delighted to meet you. Goodbye and God bless you.'*

Such a contrast to the reception that the news of his award received in his hometown. The powers that be made all the correct noises, the neighbours in Ebor Street put out the bunting for his homecoming, and there was a civic reception for him at the City Hall where a letter was read out from the Prime Minister of Northern Ireland, Sir Basil Brooke, but there is evidence that his VC was greeted by embarrassment by both sides of the political divide. It suited neither side that the only person to be awarded a VC during the war was a working class Catholic from the Falls. This did not fit in with the 'them and us' political narrative.

Much has been made of the fact that James was not awarded the Freedom of the City, and certainly in the subsequent decades of the century the lack of a public monument to him was a stain on the city. However, some of the criticism of the then Lord Mayor, Sir Crawford McCullagh, is unjust. Sir Crawford was a self-made man and he had a better understanding of a fitting reward to a

James Magennis

young Leading Seaman on a yearly pay of £92 than many of his critics. He established the Shilling Fund to raise money to give to Magennis and the amount eventually raised was £3,066, or approximately £150,000 today. This was an incredible amount of money and, had it been correctly invested, could have provided Magennis with an income for the rest of his life. The fact that it didn't is not the fault of Sir Crawford.

Still a serving Seaman, Magennis was embarrassed by the amount of money, as he felt that he had only been doing his job and many of his friends had lost their lives[10]. Instead he shared his money with his friends and family, and he married his wartime girlfriend Edna Skidmore from Barnsley in 1946.

James was still a serving sailor in the Royal Navy with three years of his service still left to run – albeit one whose VC ribbon meant that officers had to salute him. In fact he was the only rating in the Royal Navy with a VC, a point made clear from photographs of the Navy VCs at the time. He continued to serve as a diver on mini subs, *TRENCHANT* and *TANTALUS*, and to enjoy his shore leave. One trip ashore led to him being demoted for drunkenness, but in this he was neither the first nor last sailor to face disciplinary procedure for having one too many tots. In fact it was only in 1970 that the daily rum ration was stopped.

George Fleming[11] argues that he fell foul of:

> *'the petty trivialities of a peace time navy'* which trained *'men to blow up warships, to risk their lives for their country. When it is all over they want them to behave like Sunday School boys, without*

---

10. At the end of the war there were 74 British & Commonwealth submarines lying on sea-beds around the world, memorials to the 3,000 officers and rating who had given their lives. 39 men from the mini-submarine service lost their lives. Few if any of the bodies were ever recovered.

11. *Magennis VC: The story of Northern Ireland's only winner of the VC.* History Ireland, Dublin, 1998

understanding the mental pain and anguish some of them have been through.'

James was transferred back to general service in September 1947, having been medically downgraded from the submarine service due to damage to his ear drums. He finished his service in Drake Barracks, Plymouth.

By the time that he left the Navy, James and Edna were the proud parents to three sons, James, David and Paul. The family lived in a number of rented houses, a steady drain on the money that remained from the Shilling Fund. They decided to return to Belfast and settled in Carncaver Road, Castlereagh. James had a job in the Royal Navy air base at Sydenham and the family seemed to have settled. However tragedy struck shortly later when David was knocked down by a trolley bus on the Cregagh Road and died. Then James lost his job due to ill-health. All the money that he had received was gone it being reported *'He had shared it among his family and friends as unconditionally as he had received it.'* With bills mounting up he sold his VC for £75 to a dealer in Smithfield Market. Having said that he would keep it quiet the dealer announced to the local press that he was going to donate it to the Ulster Museum; there was a general outcry. Eventually the dealer, Joseph Kavanagh, returned the medal to James, but it was done in a blaze of publicity. A few years later James explained his actions in the *Daily Mail:*

> *My health broke down, I was broke and it didn't seem right to go begging from the British Legion … You can't eat a Victoria Cross. So I sold it to a dealer in Smithfield Market for £75 … What a stink it caused; what a blow-up. The world protested. I received hundreds of letters condemning me. Some were sympathetic, others rude and scurrilous. Then an influential friend [Viscount Furness] told me I must have my VC back. I don't know what went on but*

James Magennis

the dealer returned my VC to me. It leads my row of medals and there it stays.

He did lend the medal to the Ulster Museum for display but it was returned to him for the coronation of Elizabeth II in 1953. The incident soured relations with many in his hometown. Fleming comments that:

> '*It almost appeared that many people in Northern Ireland thought a Victoria Cross was an award for good behaviour or a guarantee for credit rating instead of an award for valour earned in wartime.*'

James felt that he did not fit into either side of the rival communities in Belfast and in February 1955 he and his family moved to Rossington, near Doncaster and he found a job as an electrician in the Rossington Colliery. In the late 1950s, following the birth of another son, Michael, the family moved to Bradford, where James got a job as an electrical and television engineer. Like many others in the following years he was subject to the vagaries of blue-collar employment and changed employer several times. Finally in 1986 he was made redundant due to ill-health.

James lived very quietly and it was only when he put his medals on to attend the remembrance service at the local cenotaph that he stood out. While he may have been happy to retreat into obscurity, his VC meant that he continued to receive official recognition of his bravery. There were annual VC reunions and garden parties at Buckingham Palace. In 1977, during the Queen's Silver Jubilee he was photographed wearing his medals, chatting animatedly to a relaxed and smiling Queen. In 1976 a street in Gosport was named after him[12], as was a naval building at the submarine base in Rosyth, Scotland. Just before his death he was the subject of a special first day stamp cover. He continues to be both remem-

---

12. Fourteen streets in a new housing estate were named after the submarine VC recipients.

bered and honoured by the Royal Navy to this day. Recently a new Training Pier at the Fleet Diving Squadron on Horsea Island, Portsmouth, was called Magennis Jetty and his diving suit is on display at the Imperial War Museum.

James died from acute bronchitis on 12 February 1986, aged 66. His funeral was attended by fellow VCs, and former navy colleagues. In October 1986 there was a memorial service for him in Bradford Cathedral, when a plaque was unveiled by Rear Admiral Place VC, CB, CVO, DSC which says:

> *Bradford salutes the memory of leading seaman James Joseph Magennis who for his singular bravery in the action by midget submarine XE3 against the cruiser TAKAO in the Jahore Straits, July 31, 1945, was awarded the Victoria Cross.*

And in his hometown – silence. It took another thirteen years, and a campaign by his biographer George Fleming, before a memorial was finally erected to the Belfast VC in the grounds of the City Hall at a ceremony attended by his sons.

WILLIAM THOMSON, LORD KELVIN
1824-1907
Mathematician and physicist

One of the worlds leading scientists of the 19th century, Thompson devised the absolute temperature scale, was a key contributor in formulating the second law of thermodynamics and played a key role in installing telegraph cables under the Atlantic.

Unless you have an interest in science or advanced mathematics, the chances are that you are not aware of William Thomson. However, if you have ever been on board a ship, made an international phone call, used an inkjet printer or surfed the world wide web to name only a few, then you have benefitted from the genius of this giant of science.

William Thomson was born in Belfast in 1824, one of seven children born to Margaret and James[1] Thomson. His father was a mathematics teacher in the University part of Inst[2] and both

---

1. James Thomson was born in 1786 on a farm outside Ballynahinch, Co. Down. He was 12 at the time of the battle of Ballynahinch in the 1798 United Irishmen's revolt and, according to David Lindley in *Degrees Kelvin* the family provided food for the rebels. After graduating in Mathematics at Glasgow University, he supplemented his salary from Inst by writing textbooks on a range of subjects including geography and astronomy as well as mathematical subjects. His textbooks were used as standard texts for several decades.
2. Royal Belfast Academical Institution

Famous Folk from Belfast

William and his older brother, James, attended the school. When he was 6 his mother died and then in 1832 his father accepted the appointment to the chair of Mathematics at Glasgow University and the entire family moved into the rather cramped university accommodation[3]. At first James let his eldest sons sit in on his lectures and David Lindley records in *Degrees Kelvin* that:

> *If their fellow students were surprised to see an 8 year old in their ranks they were astonished when the professor posed a difficult quest that left the class silent except for the small fair boy who jumped up from his seat pleading, "Do, papa, let me answer!"*

James and William, then aged 12 and 10, were formally enrolled in the university in 1834. Almost from the start it was clear that their only competition came from each other, with William almost always achieving the highest marks. Nor was it only in mathematics that he shone. By the age of 15 he had sat and passed all the final examinations at the university, although a misplaced fear that it would prevent him from attending Cambridge University meant that his father refused to allow him to graduate. In later life he would always assert that he was a Bachelor of Arts – in all but name.

The final summer before he started to study at Cambridge was a momentous one for William. His father decided to take the family away to Germany on holiday and one of his father's colleagues gave him a copy of Jean-Baptiste-Joseph Fourier's *The Analytical Theory of Heat*. He was immediately won over by the arguments and was horrified to find that not everyone was of a like mind. One rather vocal opponent was Phillip Kelland, the professor of mathematics at Edinburgh University. William decided to write a paper proving Fourier's theory and refuting Kelland's assertions. Most 16 year-

---

[3]. The family maintained their links with Belfast for many years. William's sister Anna lived there with her husband and children and his older brother James was the professor of civil engineering at the Queen's College, later QUB.

olds would have contented themselves with that. Instead William succeeded in getting it published in the *Cambridge Mathematical Journal* under the pseudonym of PQR. Two more papers were written and accepted for publication before he had even travelled to Cambridge to take up his place. By the time that he had completed his degree he had published a dozen mathematical papers in the *Journal*.

His time at Cambridge was not all work and no play. He threw himself into student life and was a founding member of the Cambridge University Music Society. Much to his father's dismay he bought himself a 'funny' [a type of rowing boat], which typically he adapted with improvements, but managed to convince his father that it was good for maintaining his health, thus assisting with his studies. His father was concerned that his tall, good-looking, affable young son would be seduced by the idleness that infected many of the richer students, but he needn't have worried as William's curiosity and thirst for knowledge would remain a driving force throughout his life. William won the Colquhoun Cup in 1844 for sculling, an achievement of which he remained very proud. Half a century later, shortly after being given a peerage he told one friend that winning the cup was *'better than winning in an examination.'*

Although he was beaten into second place in the wrangler competition[4] by Stephen Parkinson he did win the Smith's prize which rewarded mathematical understanding and analytical thought rather than just speed at repeating rote learnt formulae. He was so far advanced of the other candidates that one of the Smith examiners reportedly said to another, *'You and I are just about fit to mend his pens.'* Following his degree, and resisting his father's machinations

---

4. A wrangler is a student who achieves the highest marks in a series of third year mathematics examinations. It always attracted a lot of attention but was not necessarily an indication of future glory as it was largely a test of speed in applying familiar rules.

to lure him back to Glasgow, he spent a year in France were he worked with Victor Regnault, who was working on measuring the thermal properties of steam. As David Lindley[5] puts it:

> In his reading of Fourier he had come to know heat as an element of fundamental physics. Working ... with Regnault, he discovered heat as a source of motive power ... William's four and a half months in Paris in 1845 turned him from an applied mathematician into a man of science.

James Thomson was determined that his son should be appointed to the chair of the Natural Philosophy at Glasgow University, when the very elderly and frail incumbent, Dr. Meikleham should go to his heavenly reward. Many of the letters between father and son contained a report on the good doctor's health, but he stubbornly clung to life, despite being *'silent – vacant – and seems to notice little of what is going on around him'*. In the meantime William had to earn a living so, in June, he returned to Cambridge where he gave a number of lectures and was elected to a fellowship at St Peter's College. Finally, in early May 1846, Meikleham finally shuffled off the mortal coil and William, unopposed, was unanimously elected to the chair of Natural Philosophy[6]. He was 22 years old.

Living in what in many ways was a golden age of scientific advancement, William was in constant communication with other mathematician and physicists, including the largely self taught Michael Faraday. One of the leading lights in the discovery of the connections between electricity and magnetism, Faraday was very much focused on practical experimentation leaving the development of the underlying mathematical theories to others. Thomson was one of the first to develop the mathematics to support Faraday's theorems and Thomson's encouragement was instrumental in Faraday's

---

5. *Degrees Kelvin: a tale of genius and invention*, Aurum Press, 2004, London
6. He was to hold the chair for 53 years only resigning in 1899, aged 75, to *'make room for younger men.'*

Lord Kelvin

discovery in 1845 of the Faraday Effect which showed that light, magnetism and electricity are all related.

However it was at the 1847 annual meeting of the British Association for the Advancement of Science in Oxford that William made the acquaintance of a scientist whose theories would have a huge influence on William's scientific endeavours, James Prescott Joule. Although Thomson was initially skeptical of Joule's proposal of a new way of considering what heat actually was, his theories set Thomson thinking about thermodynamics, the branch of science where he was to leave his greatest legacy.

In 1848 he published a scientific paper *'On an Absolute Thermometric Scale'* in which he proposed a temperature scale where 0 was specified as the temperature below which it is impossible to cool any substance any further. Today the International System of Units has immortalized his name as the unit of measurement (Kelvin) in their specified scale for temperature.

In 1851 Thomson published his treatise *On the Dynamical Theory of Heat* which included his version of the second law of thermodynamics, one of science's most important and overarching laws which is thought to apply to every physical process anywhere in the universe –

> *'It is impossible, by means of inanimate material agency, to derive mechanical effect from any portion of matter by cooling it below the temperature of the coldest of the surrounding objects.'*

I must confess that my knowledge of physics is limited to an O level and that the meaning Thomson's statement does not leap out at me. Perhaps a clearer explanation of what Thomson was theorizing was provided by Quentin Cooper on BBC Radio 4's *Material World* who explained that if the first law of thermodynamics is that you can't get something for nothing, then the second law is that you can't even break even [which incidentally makes the construction of a perpetual motion machine impossible].

Although Thomson made an enormous contribution in the field of thermodynamics he also contributed to many other fields of scientific endeavour. Such was the breadth of his work that quite frankly it would be impossible to examine each of his discoveries in depth in a short biography given that by the time of his death William had published 661 scientific papers and had 75 patents for his inventions.

Interestingly, despite his huge achievements in pure science and mathematics, the activity for which he was awarded his knighthood in 1866 was not for his achievements in these fields but was due to his involvement in the Atlantic Telegraph Company as an engineer and scientific advisor.

Telegraphy was not a new science and there were even some short cables across both the Irish Sea and the English Channel, however most people thought that there was no prospect of extending a cable across the Atlantic Ocean. Cyrus Field, an American businessman, disagreed. He had made a fortune in paper and now wanted a new venture. Having failed to attract any investors in his native land, but having secured landing rights in Newfoundland, he travelled to England in 1856 where he rapidly raised £350,000 to finance his idea to lay a telegraph cable from Valencia in Ireland to America. Cables at the time were made from twisted copper wires which were covered in gutta percha [7], then wrapped in tarred hemp and finally wrapped with iron wires. Leaving aside the physical challenge of laying the cables, and there were to be four failed attempts before this was achieved, there was a greater problem. While over short distances the signals came through loud and

---

7. Gutta percha is a tree sap from Malaysia. It is similar to rubber but has better insulating properties and longevity under water.

clear, the longer the cable the more the signal was distorted until eventually it became indecipherable. This distortion was called retardation and Field consulted Michael Faraday to see if there was a solution to the problem. Faraday, in turn consulted both William and George Gabriel Stokes[8]. Over a series of letters William eventually calculated the optimal cable design to allow the signal rate (today known as bandwidth) to be increased to the point where it would be commercially viable.

This is where William differed from many of his contemporaries. Not only had he applied his scientific knowledge to solve the problem but he also recognised the commercial application of his solution. In 1854, together with his brother James and a friend, he applied for his first patent, to protect his discovery. While this initial patent didn't make them much money, subsequent ones were to amass him a fortune.

However the road to success was not entirely smooth and a stumbling block arose in the form of the wonderfully named Edward Orange Wildman Whitehouse who had also been working on a solution to the Retardation problem and had been appointed Chief Electrician to the Atlantic Telegraph Company. Much older than Thomson and jealous of the younger man's genius, Whitehouse stubbornly stuck to his own findings and solutions. While Whitehouse was a paid employee of the company, William was appointed to the Board of Directors and was not compensated for his work.

The first attempt at laying a cable in the summer of 1857 was not a success and was quickly abandoned when the apparatus for

---

8. George Gabriel Stokes was the youngest son of a Church of Ireland clergyman from Sligo. He was a lifelong friend and colleague of William Thomson and their long correspondence on matters scientific was to lead to both being remembered as scientific pioneers. He was appointed Lucasian Professor of Mathematics at Cambridge in 1849 and held it until his death in 1903.

reeling the cable off the ship was found to be not fit for purpose. Whitehouse was supposed to be on board the ship but William took his place when the older man claimed to be too ill to travel. The initial results before the attempt was abandoned had convinced William that there was a problem with both the design of the cable and delivery of the signal so before the next attempt the following summer he devised a new design for the cable (which was 2mm in diameter) and in 1858 he patented his mirror galvanometer[9], a sensitive piece of apparatus to sense the weak signals which made it through the cable. It also proved to be very successful at detecting any defects in the core of the cable both during its manufacture and when submerged at great depths.

Further attempts were made in the summer of 1858, and despite two failures, by the 5th August, the effort appeared to have succeeded. Yet again Whitehouse had cried off the voyage and so William was on board the *Agamemnon* when it arrived it Valencia. When Field, in Newfoundland, telegraphed the news to his native New York, it was greeted with great celebration including church bells pealing, bonfires and even sermons from the pulpit. However it was a bit premature. William had been instructed to deliver his precious cargo into the hands of Whitehouse in Ireland. Whitehouse, determined that he knew better, immediately disconnected William's sensitive mirror galvanometer and attached a heavier version of his own devising. Whitehouse's equipment was much less sensitive than William's and in an effort to make it work he applied some 2,000 volts to the sensitive copper wire, frying it in the process. When the truth emerged the company decided that it could do without his services and he returned to Brighton an embittered man. It is to William's credit that until he was confronted with the incontrovertible truth about Whitehouse's actions, he tried to de-

---

9. William Thomson did not invent the mirror galvanometer. His patent is an improved version, developed specifically to work with the transatlantic cable.

Lord Kelvin

fend him and save his position in the company. It is doubtful that Whitehouse would have returned the favour if the boot had been on the other foot.

It was to be several years before Field was once more able to raise the capital needed to make another attempt. William was not idle during the break. 1861 he joined a British Association committee with other leading scientists including Joule, Wheatstone and James Clerk Maxwell[10] to investigate the optimum electrical voltages, currents and message structure for use in telegraphy. He tried to impress upon his colleagues the importance of understanding electrical tests in a sound theoretical way as well as through experience. His affable personality and ability to see both sides of the argument is illustrated at this time by the fact that when he broke his leg and was unable to attend meetings for a number of months, proceedings broke down in acrimony.

By the mid 1860s, Field was again in a position to make another attempt on a trans-Atlantic cable many of the earlier problems had been ironed out, largely thanks to Thomson's continuing improvements not only with the cable itself but also the mechanism to lay it. On the 23 July 1865, with William on board as a scientific advisor, the *Great Eastern,* stripped back to its basics to make room for the massive drums of cable, set sail from Ireland. Despite early problems with the paying out machinery everything seemed to be going well until, just 600 miles away from Newfoundland the cable snapped and disappeared 2,500 fathoms down into the Atlantic. Four attempts were made to grapple the cable to the surface but each failed and so they had to return to shore.

---

10. James Clerk Maxwell was a renowned mathematician and physicist. He is widely regarded as the father of modern quantum mechanics. He and Thomson were life long friends and both had similar personalities, although Maxwell was often bullied by his tyrannical wife Katherine who once brought a social gathering at Cambridge to an end by announcing "James, it's time you went home, you are beginning to enjoy yourself."

Famous Folk from Belfast

Unlike the previous attempts in the 1850s this time Field, Thomson and the other directors and investors had reason to be hopeful. Until it had disappeared into the deep the cable had been working perfectly. The following year on, of all days, Friday 13th of July the *Great Eastern* set off from Ireland and on Saturday 28 July it reached the small fishing village of Heart's Content in Newfoundland. More importantly the signal was coming through loud and clear. Buoyed up by the success Thomson set out back across the Atlantic to try to find and retrieve the broken cable from the previous year. In the intervening months he had worked with the other engineers to devise a scheme whereby the strain of lifting the cable would be shared between 3 ships. On 2 September they succeeded and there were now two transatlantic telegraph wires in place. The world had just shrunk.

It is impossible to overstate the importance of this achievement. In 1814 the battle of New Orleans was fought between the British and the Americans, two months after the peace Treaty of Ghent had been signed, simply because it took that long for the news to travel across the ocean. Now it would take a matter of minutes. Soon the same technology was used to circle the globe. Almost all of the cables were built, laid and operated with equipment designed, patented and in many cases manufactured by William Thomson and the firms he controlled. This was in fact the start of the digital revolution and the Internet. David Saxon, Kelvin Professor of Physics at Glasgow University, says that all the logic features of email were present in Thomson's telegraphy – it was digitally encoded, package switched and the operator found the best route.

In 1867 Thomson's inventive mind led him to take out a patent on a new instrument that he called a siphon recorder. It used electrostatic forces to apply ink to paper and 'printed' wobbly lines of ink which could be translated into letters and words. Its direct descendant is the modern ink-jet printer.

Lord Kelvin

His trips on board the telegraph ships had reignited his love of the sea and following the death of his wife Margaret, who had enjoyed ill-health throughout their 17 year marriage; he had the freedom and financial means to indulge his love of the sea. In 1870 he bought the 126 ton, 17 year old *Lalla Rookh*, which was to become his mobile home for the rest of his life. As Lindley notes:

> *'He threw himself into sailing with the same energy he used to attack any scientific, technical commercial problem that came his way.'*

For example while sailing in the Bay of Biscay he started experiments to improve sounding devices. Frustrated with having to wait for the tide he developed a rudimentary analog computer to work out tides, which could and did work throughout the world. He tried to explain through mathematics the behaviour of waves. The resulting formulae describing what is today known as a Kelvin Wave is currently progressing the work of meteorologist and oceanographers to predict weather events such as El Nino and continues to change the way we model climates and oceans. Confronted with the problems of operating a traditional compass on a metal ship he designed a new compass, which was bought by the Admiralty and all manufacturers of metal ships, including Harland and Wolff.

The list is endless. Perhaps, as is the wont of people as they get older, he did become a little stuck in his ways in later life and people are quick to point out that he said that *'the aeroplane is scientifically impossible'*, *'Radio has no future'*, and *'X-rays are clearly a hoax'*. It should however be pointed out that he was willing to be convinced otherwise and even had his own hand x-rayed towards the end of his life. He also came up against the new emerging theories of evolution as he was unable to accept that his calculation for the age of the earth was wrong[11].

---

11. His mathematics were not wrong but the underlying physical theories were – convection in the earth's mantle, energy released in radioactive decay and the processes by which the sun generates its energy were all unknown factors at the time

Famous Folk from Belfast

Another criticism leveled against him, even when he was alive, was that he might have taken credit for the work of others. This is to misunderstand the way in which he and his fellow scientists worked. Theirs was always a collaborative process, with letters containing formulae, musings and criticisms flying between the various universities. Maxwell might pose a question and Peter Guthrie Tait[12] might solve it or, as happened, Thomson might share a formulae and Maxwell might set it as an exam question thus associating with himself. Thomson's work on establishing Absolute Zero was based on the work of his predecessors in the field, namely Faraday, Carnot and Regnault. Just in the same way in which Albert Einstein in the twentieth century built on some of Thomson's work to derive the pithier $E=mc^2$. Are we to dismiss Einstein's work because it was influenced and informed by others?

Throughout his life William had had the ability to charm and enchant. He didn't have any children but when he died, on the 17 December 1907, he was surrounded by his loving nephews and nieces. He was survived by his second wife Frances Blandy. His body was taken from his Ayrshire home and, with great pomp and circumstances, interred in Westminster Abbey beside Sir Issac Newton.

In a letter to Robert Hooke, Sir Issac Newton wrote *'If I have seen further it is by standing on the shoulders of giants.'* For those that came after him wee Willie Thomson from Belfast was one such giant.

---

12. Peter Guthrie Tait, Professor of Natural Philosophy at Edinburgh University is best known for the knot theory. Google it as I don't understand it!

CHAIM HERZOG
1918-1997

6th President of Israel, diplomat, soldier, lawyer

Chaim Herzog was born in Belfast although he spent most of his formative years in Dublin. Serving in the British army in WW2 he was exposed to the horrors of the Holocaust and became an ardent Zionist. He played a key role in the establishment of the state of Israel serving as its president fro 1983 to 1993

Chaim Herzog was born in Belfast on 17 September 1918, into an Orthodox Jewish Rabbinical family. Not only was his father a rabbi, but so too were both his grandfathers. On his mother's side a long line of rabbis could trace their family back to the time of the Old Testament.[1] Their extended family was scattered throughout Europe and what was then the United Kingdom of Great Britain and Ireland. Many of them had fled from the pogroms of Czarist Russia and found refuge in the capitals of Western Europe. While Chaim was still a baby, the family moved to Dublin where his father, Issac, had been appointed as Chief Rabbi of the small Irish Jewish community.

---

1. When Chaim's wife, Aura, told Elizabeth II about his maternal descent from King David the queen said that she was supposed to be descended from King David too. "Welcome to the family" replied Aura. *Living History: A Memoir*

Famous Folk from Belfast

The Dublin that Chaim grew up in was a city in the middle of political unrest as the Irish War of Independence, and later Civil War, was played out on the streets. In his autobiography, *Living History: A Memoir*, he remembers seeing a man being shot dead outside their house when he was only 3 years old. As a committed Zionist, Chaim's father, Issac was sympathetic with the republican desire for self-determination and a land of their own. He was fluent in Irish and was a personal friend of many in the vanguard of the creation of a newly independent state. Eamon De Valera was a frequent guest at their home, with Robert Briscoe[2] and in 1950 was one of the first foreign statesmen to visit the new state of Israel, dining with Robert Briscoe at Isaac's home in Jerusalem. As Chief Rabbi, Issac also maintained good relations with the heads of the other religions. Chaim recalled later how at one state dinner his father was seated beside Cardinal McRory, the primate of all Ireland. Due to his religion's strict dietary laws, the only dish that Issac was able to eat was the fruit and *'the cardinal reproached him for not trying the excellent ham being offered. My father ... smiled whimsically and said, "let us discuss this at your wedding."'*

While he always retrained both an affection for his childhood home, and traces of his Dublin accent his closest relations lived in England and France, and with personal experience of the inherent danger of living as Jews in an increasingly anti-Semitic Europe, they were all committed Zionists.

When his paternal grandfather, Rabbi Joel Leib Herzog, died in Paris the family wanted to take his body to be buried in Jerusalem

---

2. Robert Briscoe was the son of Lithuanian Jews who had escaped Russian pogroms to settle in Dublin. One of his brothers was called Wolfe Tone Briscoe. He was sent, by Michael Collins, to Germany to buy arms for the IRA although he fought for the Anti-Treaty side in the Civil War. He acted as a special advisor to Menachem Begin, and gave guerilla warfare tactical training to members of Irgun, a Zionist paramilitary organisation in British Mandate Palestine.

as a result of which Chaim first visited the country that was to be his future home on 15 May 1935.

His maternal grandparents had already moved to Jerusalem and Chiam decided to follow them and enter the Yeshivot [religious school] and complete his Talmudic education. He initially stayed with a German doctor, his wife and her mother. The elderly lady didn't speak any language other than German, which he was able to add to his growing lexicon of languages. This family was one of many who had sought safety in British Mandatory Palestine fleeing from the increasingly dangerous anti-Semite laws of Nazi Germany.

I feel it is important to pause here to explain the situation in the area between the world wars. The Ottoman Empire been in control since the 16th century buturing the First World War an Arab uprising[3], combined with the British Egyptian Expeditionary Force under General Allenby drove them out of Sinai and Palestine. This led to the British and the French establishing a joint 'Occupied Enemy Territory Administration' in Syria and dividing the area up into 'spheres of influence'. Britain obtained a mandate from the newly established League of Nations[4] in 1922 to administer Palestine *'until such times as they are able to stand alone.'* This allowed the three main communities already resident in the area to continue to operate their own courts for marriage, divorce, inheritance etc, while the British administered the rest. The British Mandate only came to an end in 1949 with the partition of the territory into Israel, Arab West Bank [annexed by the Kingdom of Jordan] and the Arab All-Palestine Protectorate in the Gaza Strip [under the control of Egypt]. Added into this rather complicated situation of competing religious communities was the 1917 Balfour Declaration which stated:

---

3. Think Lawrence of Arabia.
4. Forerunner of the United Nations

Famous Folk from Belfast

> 'His majesty's government view with favour the establishment in Palestine of a national homeland for the Jewish people and will use their best endeavours to facilitate the achievement of this object, it being clearly understood that nothing shall be done which may prejudice the civil and religious rights of existing non-Jewish communities in Palestine.'

No sooner had Chaim settled in to his new home and school than the country was gripped by the Arab Revolt. This was a nationalist uprising against not only the British administration but also against what they saw as officially 'tolerated' Jewish immigration and subsequent land purchases[5]. The uprising, one of several during the British Mandate[6] was accompanied by attacks on Jewish families and property. Jewish society at the time felt that the British authorities were pro-Arab and slow to defend the Jewish community and several underground movements had emerged to both protect the community and prepare for an independent Jewish state[7]. The main groups were the Haganah, the Irgun and the Stern group.

The Haganah had approximately 40,000 members and was led by David Ben-Gurion and Chaim joined them as soon as he was old enough. No doubt influenced by the conversations with De Valera and Briscoe he had heard in Dublin home, he recalled:

> 'the overwhelming sense that the possibility of impending statehood meant that one could and <u>should</u> finally fight for this ultimate

---

5. Many of the Jewish immigrants flowing into the country from Germany were professional families who had been able to liquidize their assets and so were able to buy property and land in the Mandatory area.

6. In riots in Hebron in 1929, Chaim's maternal great-grandmother (aged 80) was seriously injured by Arab rioters, who killed the other 17 people sheltering with her, only escaping death by pretending to be dead.

7. The Irgun, later led by Mencahem Begin, had received paramilitary training from Robert Briscoe in Ireland and was on the right politically. The Stern Group was a breakaway group from Irgun. Both of these groups were quite small.

dream. One could no longer be outside the pale and expect to be part of the new state.'

He was given military training and then assigned to a company responsible for the protection of a particular area against Arab attack.

By this time Chaim's parents had also moved to Palestine after Isaac had been elected Chief Rabbi[8] and, in addition to his studies and Haganah patrols, Chaim was expected to help his father as an unofficial personal secretary. Alarmed by the effect this was having on his education his parents decided that he should go to the University of London to study Law. In the summer of 1938 he travelled to London, via Paris where he spent time with his Aunt Esther and her family. It was to be the last time that he would see his cousin Annette, who he would learn in summer 1942 had been sent to Auschwitz[9].

After his graduation in 1941[10] he immediately volunteered for the British Army and was sent for basic training. In his autobiography he said:

'I was there to fight the German Nazis; as a Jew I perhaps understood more than anyone else in my unit the significance of the struggle for which we were preparing ourselves. I was a soldier now – and happy to be one.'

It was during this basic training that he received his nickname 'Vivian' when the NCOs could not pronounce his Hebrew name[11].

---

8. Chaim notes that having *"grown up in a Western atmosphere, [he] had observed the institutions set up in a new state of Ireland …[it] had left its mark on him"*.
9. His aunt and another cousin were hidden by friends and survived the war.
10. He was called to the bar on 17 November 1942.
11. Chaim, means 'life', the English equivalent is Vivian.

Famous Folk from Belfast

In February 1943 he was transferred to the Intelligence Corps Training Depot in Wentworth Woodhouse, Yorkshire, and then in June 1943 to the Royal Military College in Aldershot. In September 1943, he received his commission and was promoted to second lieutenant. His training in military intelligence continued with a number of postings and courses. He noted that:

> '*One of the things I observed was that painful treatment frequently strengthened a prisoner's resolve not to divulge accurate information ...[which] later proved useful when I interrogated Hitler Youth and SS officers. Having grown up with a deep hatred of their enemy, they expected to be martyred, to be treated as they had been trained to deal with prisoners. But when they were questioned with humanity, the shock of it often led to a grateful flow of information.*'

He said that it was a lesson that he would take with him in his future career in the new state of Israel.

One of his postings was to take him back to Belfast, where, as an intelligence officer on the staff of Lieutenant General Sir Alan Cunningham [later the last British High Commissioner in Palestine] he worked with the first American divisions who were posted to Northern Ireland, in preparation for the invasion of Europe. When off-duty he visited the house where he was born and fought off determined attempts to marry him off to '*attractive girls in the community*'.

A month after D-Day he was sent to France where he was attached to the Guards Armoured Division which in early September reached Brussels. On leave he visited Paris where he was reunited with his aunt and met other Jews who had survived the Nazi occupation.

> '*Listening to their stories, I realised the importance of the national home and independent state that we dreamed of and prayed for. I resolved to make every sacrifice to achieve that independence.*'

Chaim Herzog

That resolve was to harden as he stood in a small concentration camp just outside Bremen.

> *'It was a terrifying sight, one I will never forget. ... I smelled the rotting corpses of the Jews, the Gypsies and Poles.'*

Later he visited Bergen-Belsen, just after its liberation and after the German surrender he was sent to join a small team of interrogation officers based at Barfeld who were trying to uncover all the Nazi leaders who had gone into hiding. It was here that he came face to face with Heinrich Himmler, commander of the SS and one of the main architects of the Final Solution. Chaim remembered that:

> *'I saw Himmler only briefly and heard him say only a few words. Out of his gleaming Nazi uniform he looked like a drab and unimposing clerk, the kind of man we pass every day in the street.'*

Of all his wartime experiences, the one which was to have the most important effect on the course of his life was working as a yiddish translator at a conference of Jewish displaced persons held in the British Zone at Bergen-Bergen under the auspices of Field Marshal Montgomery and General Templer.

The main problem to emerge from the conference was that, while the Allies wanted the displaced Jews to return to their European homes, the Jews themselves did not. Jewish survivors of the slave labour and concentration camps saw that their former homes either no longer existed or were held by, often hostile, former neighbours. For every neighbour who had risked their own lives saving or hiding their Jewish friends there were hundreds who had actively reported them to the Nazis or had said nothing as they were stripped of their rights, their properties and their lives. As such they had no desire to return, but wanted to leave and find safety in Britain, America or Palestine and were determined to be seen as a separate entity, rather than as citizens of the countries they had lived in prewar. They had been persecuted because of their religious identity, not their nationality.

At the end of 1946, Chaim was demobbed and decided to return to Palestine. The Jerusalem that he returned to was very tense, especially in the wake of the bombing of the King David Hotel[12] and continuing attacks on troops by Arabs and Jews alike. Chaim remembered feeling a huge conflict - like many in Ireland in 1918 one minute he was a British Army officer, the next he was on the opposite side.

In the summer of 1947 the Labour Foreign Secretary, Ernest Bevin[13], announced that Britain had decided to withdraw from Palestine and pass the region over to the newly formed United Nations. Chaim was asked by the leadership of Haganah to set up a department to monitor UNSCOP[14].

On 29 November 1947 the General Assembly of the United Nations voted by a ratio of 33:13, with 10 abstentions, to create a new state of Israel[15]. British withdrawal was set for May 1948, and the UN set up a special commission to transfer power to the new Jewish and Arab states. As the date set for withdrawal approached, Chaim was appointed deputy head of the Jewish Agency's Security Department and was responsible for direct liaison between the Jewish and British authorities as Arab attacks on Jewish settlements

---

12. King David Hotel in Jerusalem housed the offices of the Palestine government and also acted as military headquarters for the British. The Irgun had smuggled bombs concealed in milk cans into one wing of the hotel and the resulting explosion had killed 98 people, civilians as well as military, Jews, Arabs and Christians.

13. Bevin is best known as the father of the NHS.

14. United Nations Special Committee on Palestine

15. The UN resolution recommended the creation of independent Arab and Jewish States and a Special International Regime for the city of Jerusalem. The Partition Plan, a four-part document attached to the resolution, provided for the termination of the Mandate, the progressive withdrawal of British armed forces and the delineation of boundaries between the two States and Jerusalem.

increased in intensity. Both he and his wife Aura were injured in a bomb attack on the Jewish Agency building in Jerusalem as the Arab Legion's offensive against the Jewish quarter of Jerusalem intensified. By the time of the Passover in 1948 the city was besieged and his father's appeals to *'the Christian religious leaders worldwide to rally support against the profaning of Jerusalem'* were met with a deafening silence. Tasked with trying to negotiate a ceasefire, Chaim was in constant contact with foreign embassies, who acted as go-betweens with the Arab leaders. In his autobiography he remembers being in the French consulate as:

> *'Bullets came through the open windows. Madame Neuville [the consul's wife] remained calm throughout the proceedings and even brought a makeshift meal for those in our negotiating room. Despite the extreme danger, she did not forget to serve a good French wine. Avoiding the bullets, she crawled on the floor to serve it.'*

For the second time of his life, the Herzog family were involved in a War of Independence, with Chaim taking an active role in the relief of the beleaguered Jerusalem community.

His experience in the British army saw him being appointed as deputy head of the new state's military intelligence department. He was determined that by using the very latest technology he:

> *'had to create a situation in which Israel would never be taken by surprise. To ensure our very existence, we had to always be several steps ahead of our hostile neighbours',*

The Israel Defense team had only three full-time brigades which the Arab Legion had twenty-four. Finally on 14 February 1949 an armistice agreement was signed with Egypt, followed by one with Lebanon on 23 March, with Transjordan on 3 April, and finally Syria on 20 July.

Chaim was sent to Washington as a defence representative attached to the new embassy. This was at the height of the communist conspiracy, McCarthy trails and he recounted how the arrival of his baby son Joel in New York, accompanied by his nanny, gave him a personal experience of the paranoia at the time:

> ' ... *Joel, who was travelling on a separate diplomatic passport, had not signed a statement required by the MacCarran Act declaring that he was not then nor had he ever been a member of the Communist Party. That he was nine months old was of no concern to the immigration officers – if he couldn't sign the loyalty oath he couldn't enter the country.*'

Despite American concerns that some of the recent Jewish immigrants came from communist European states, Chaim managed to secure State Department aid to Israel, as well as gaining admittance for Israeli students to US armed forces training colleges. The military coup in Egypt by Nasser, actually worked in his favour as the Soviet Union supplied arms to the new regime. Israel was now seen as a vital pawn in the wider Cold War.

His time in Washington was not exclusively spent nurturing closer relations with the West's leading super-power. He also developed close personal relations with many of the leading Arab diplomats, much to the displeasure of their leaders and, to be honest, his own. He also established close links to the American Jewish community, helping to launch the Israel bond campaign[16] He also argued, largely in vain, that the Israeli government should try to use public relations to at least try to make friends with the rest of the world. Despite his best efforts the government refused to accept the invitation to join the Western Europe and Others bloc in the United Nations, thus meaning that they didn't belong to any bloc and were never given a seat on the Security Council, and were ineligible for appointments to various UN committees. This was to have

---

16. The Israel bonds campaign allowed Israel to borrow money while guaranteeing repayment with interest. He notes that *'Over the years, Israel has borrowed billions through bonds – and paid back every cent.'*

Chaim Herzog

a detrimental effect and to lead to one of the reasons why Chaim Herzog is still remembered today.

During his time in Washington he frequently met up with friends from his old home in Ireland, including Robert Briscoe, then Lord Mayor of Dublin. Briscoe invited him to a dinner in Boston and, pointing at Herzog, opened his speech with, *'There was once an Irishman and a Jew, and here he is.'* When John Hearne, Ambassador of Ireland discovered that his military attaché was unable to attend the St Patrick's Day party, he phoned Chaim and asked him to attend in full Israeli Defense Force uniform, saying that *'Sure, nobody will know the difference, and at least you speak Gaelic.'* Chaim also came face to face with the racial segregation laws and anti-Jewish discrimination, once being turned down for a rented home when the owners discovered that he was attached to the Israeli embassy.

Herzog returned to Israel in 1954, where he served in various military posts until he was recalled to Military Intelligence in 1959 where he worked to upgrade the intelligence gathering capability of the organisation leading to it becoming one of the first in the world to become computerized. He also worked with the Shah's regime in Iran, as they were one of Israel's only friends among the Muslim nations. In his autobiography he is very critical of the human rights abuses and rampant corruption which occurred under the Shah but says that, *'Sometimes that's what politics seems to boil down to: the choice of a rational evil over an irrational one'.*

In 1958, shortly before his father died, he accompanied him back to Ireland, where a forest was being planted in his honour.

After retiring from the army in 1962 he returned to practice law, but returned to the public sphere when he made a series of radio broadcasts during the Six Day war in 1967. He was much in demand as a military commentator with foreign broadcasters such as the BBC, as much with the local radio station. With his intimate knowledge of the country's defence capabilities he is did his best to reassure the civilian population:

> 'If I had to choose tonight between being an Egyptian pilot attacking Tel Aviv and being a citizen in the city of Tel Aviv, I would in the interest of self-preservation prefer to be in the city of Tel Aviv.'

Following the end of the war he was appointed military governor of the West Bank but his return to the military was short lived and he soon returned to the civilian world of law and commerce, working for GUS-Rassco before setting up the law firm of Herzog & Fox in 1972.

While he may have thought that he had done enough for his nation, he was brought back into public life in 1975 when he was appointed as the Israeli ambassador to the United Nations in New York. Over a decade earlier he had tried to advise the then leadership of Israel of their short-sightedness in rejecting the offer to join the Western bloc in the UN and he was there to witness the outcome of their intransigence.

Almost from the creation of the nation, Herzog had been urging political leaders from all sides of the political divide in Israel, to pay attention to public relations outside their borders and away from their own electorate, but largely to no avail. He argued that there was no point in making offers of concessions to the neighbouring Arab nations in secret, while allowing the same nations free rein in the UN. They were winning the propaganda war despite the fact that their human rights records were appalling and democracy was non-existent. This failure to engage in PR came to a climax in the UN on 10 November 1975 when the General Assembly debated Resolution 3379 that:

'determined that Zionism is a form of racism and racial discrimination'.

During the debate before the vote, Herzog made a speech that is regularly recognised as one of the greatest speeches of the twentieth century. If you have the time, and irrespective of your views about Israel and Zionism, I would encourage you to look for it on YouTube. During the course of the speech he reminded the Assembly that it was the 37th anniversary of Kristallnacht:

> "It is indeed ironic, Mr President, that the UN, which began its life as an anti-Nazi alliance, should thirty years later find itself on its way to becoming the world centre of anti-Semitism. Hitler would have felt at home."

Reminding the Assembly that Judaism was the religion that has given the world the human values of the Bible, and was the source of three major religions, he continued:

> "I do not come to this rostrum to defend the moral and historical values of the Jewish people. They do not need to be defended. They speak for themselves.
>
> I come to denounce the two great evils which menace society in general and a society of nations in particular. These two great evils are hatred and ignorance ... These two evils characterize those who would drag this world organization, the ideals of which were first conceived by the prophets of Israel, to the depths to which it has been dragged today."

Contrasting the democracy of Israel with the despotism in its Arab neighbours, the freedom of worship of all religions in Israel with the theocratic intolerance of its Arab nations, and with his Irish accent becoming more pronounced as he was caught up in the emotion of the event, he continued:

> "Zionism is the name of the national movement of the Jewish people and ... is to the Jewish people what the liberation movements of Africa and Asia have been to their own people ... it is based on a unique and unbroken connection, extending for four thousand years, between the People of the Book and the Land of the Bible.

Famous Folk from Belfast

I stand here not as a supplicant. Vote as your moral conscience dictates to you ...

For us, the Jewish people, this is but a passing episode in a rich and event-filled history. We put our trust in our Providence, in our faith and beliefs in our time-hallowed tradition, in our striving for social advance and human values, and in our people wherever they may be. For us the Jewish people, this resolution based on hatred, falsehood and arrogance is devoid of any moral or legal value. For us the Jewish people, this is no more than a piece of paper and we will treat it as such."

With that he tore the resolution in half and returned to his seat. The resolution was passed by a ratio of 72:35 (with 32 abstentions). Ireland, the land of his birth, was one of the 35 to vote against.

When he was recalled to Israel, he returned to private life, before entering the Knessett (the Israeli parliament) as a Labor MP before he was elected as the sixth President of Israel in 1983. He was determined that he was going to be a President of all the people of Israel, Jew, Arab or Christian, and his two terms as President were remarkable for his willingness to engage with and assist the non-Jewish population, making the first visit to Nazareth by an Israeli President.

As President he increased the number of state visits, including being the first President of Israel to make an official visit to West Germany in 1987. The visit was controversial in Israel, but he argued that the return of a Jewish President of Israel would be a *moment of victory over the criminals who had perpetrated the Holocaust.'* His state visit started with a ceremony at Bergen-Belsen, where forty years previously he had stood in the newly liberated camp, trying to comprehend the horror he was witnessing.

Earlier in his Presidency he had made a state visit in June 1985 to Ireland. In preparation for the visit he enlisted the help of the Irish commander of the UNIFIL Forces in Lebanon to assist him

Chaim Herzog

in brushing up his Gaelic. Each of his speeches in Ireland started with a greeting in both Hebrew and Gaelic, much to the delight of his hosts. It was as much a homecoming as a state visit. He was accompanied not only by his wife but also his niece, Shira and delighted in showing them his early childhood home.

Chaim Herzog was not a plaster saint. He was a man with all the failings of men, but he tried to do good. A life long liberal, he always tried to ensure that the country he had helped to create would be inclusive, not exclusive; educated, not ignorant; forward looking, not constantly looking to past wrongs. His experiences immediately after the Second World War, shaped the solider, diplomat, politician and President that he became. He believed that *'it is much easier to hate and kill a disembodied enemy than a person who appears to be human and normal'* and he constantly sought to maintain dialogue with his nation's enemies. He was always aware of the dangers of fundamentalism, whether it was religious or political. I cannot think of another family who were actively involved in the birth of not one but two new nations, but the Herzogs helped to shape both Israel and Ireland. He never forgot his Irish roots, and would always seek out 'fellow Irishmen' wherever he went in the world. He tried to shape a liberal, modern outward looking society and remained optimistic until the end. There are many who will condemn him nowadays for his Zionism, but he would argue that it was born out of the anti-Semitism of the European past and while he forged relations with the modern German nation he could never forget the sight or the smell of *'the rotting corpses of the Jews, the Gypsies and Poles'* in the liberated camps in 1945.

Chaim Herzog died in Tel Aviv on 17 April 1997 and is buried on Mount Herzl, Jerusalem.

Zikhrono livrakha.

Jack Kyle O.B.E.
1926-2014
Surgeon, Rugby Player

Kyle was a key player in the Irish rugby team which won the Grand Slam in 1948, a feat not emulated for 61 years. After the 1950 Lions tour of New Zealand he was listed as one of the top five players in the world.

While I was writing my *Famous Folk from Co. Down* book I put up a good, but ultimately futile argument to my publisher for the inclusion of a rugby player. I was informed that his connection with Co. Down was tenuous and so I conceded, temporarily. However, when the suggestion was made for a new volume in the series, this time concerning the city up the road there could no longer be any debate. So, I am delighted to recount that one of my life-long sporting heroes was born and played his club rugby in Belfast. Jack Kyle.

The reason why I know next to nothing about association football is because I have spent most of my life watching rugby football. I attended my first rugby match at the tender age of six weeks old and it is a passion that is still with me undisclosed years later.

Jack Kyle

For most of my life I heard stories about Dr Jack Kyle, the Scarlet Pimpernel of Irish rugby and a member of the only team to win the Grand Slam, who gave it all up to practice his medicine as a surgeon in rural Zambia. Then in 2009 the impossible dream became a reality and Ireland, finally, won another Grand Slam. There are so many memories of the glorious day. Jim Neilly abandoning all pretence of impartiality when Tommy Bowe scored his try, '*Holy God in Heaven! What a try by Tommy Bowe!*' The final, heart-stopping seconds of the game when Stephen Jones missed a penalty for Wales. But an image that remains as clear as all the rest is the photo of Brian O'Driscoll, the Irish captain, smiling into the eyes and clutching the hands of a beaming elderly, white-haired gentleman, Jack Kyle.

If you had ever had the privilege to meet Jack, you would never have known you were in the presence of a sporting legend. Such was his modesty about his sporting achievements that his own daughter, Justine, was bemused when people would come over and shake his hand. When, in 1991, her father was awarded an honorary degree at Queen's University Belfast she recalls:

> "*as I listened to the citation being read, I began to wonder who this person was they were talking about. I didn't know about the many awards he had received ... or about the real extent of his rugby prowess. I hadn't realized how much he was admired.*"

That she should have been unaware of the extent of his brilliance is understandable when he said of himself that:

> "*I threw a piece of leather about half a century ago. It's amazing and flattering that anybody remembers at all, to be quite truthful.*"

Jack was born on 10th February 1926, one of two sons and three daughters born to John and Elizabeth Kyle. His father was the Irish manager of the North British Rubber Company, who helped develop a way of producing specially coated wire which was used

Famous Folk from Belfast

to demagnetize [degauss] ships to reduce the likelihood of them setting off magnetic mines. During WW2 he had over 100 men at Harland & Wolffe's shipyard working for him and used to take the young Jack and his older brother Eric to the shipyard to oversee the work. The family lived in a largish house on Glenburn Park, off Old Westland Road and attended Fortwilliam Presbyterian Church. Jack had a normal, happy home life, with family holidays in Whitehead, Portstewart and Portrush, as well as day-trips to Tyrella Beach, Newcastle for picnics, where the four older children would organize races up and down the shoreline. All of the children were naturally talented at sport and one of Jack's sisters, Betty, went on to captain the Irish Ladies Hockey Team when they won the Triple Crown in 1950, while his older brother Eric would play with Jack on the Ulster Rugby team in the 1950s. However, sport was very much seen as a recreation and both his parents placed greater value on a good education and academic success.

At the age of 4 Jack was enrolled at the Belfast Royal Academy and was to remain at the school for the remainder of his education. He was a diligent rather than an outstanding academic student and achieved a perfect attendance record throughout his time at the school. The Headmaster at the time was Alec Foster who had captained Ireland from 1910 to 1912 and toured South Africa with the British Isles [Lions] team in 1910. It was unsurprising that there was a good sports department at the school under his leadership and both Jack and his older brother Eric represented the school for both rugby and cricket as well as boxing and taking part in athletics. Jack won the school's Althletics Cup and held the record for the Long Jump. In both 1943 and 1944 Jack played for the Ulster Schoolboys XV against Leinster. He later recalled that:

> *"I loved all sports and played any and every sport I could. I remember the first time I played rugby. The coach ordered me into the scrum but I hated the aggressive contact nature of the position I was in. After that game, I decided that the scrum was the last place in*

the world I ever intended to be again, so I asked the coach if I could play at full-back. Luckily, he agreed, and I played in that position up to my first year in the First XV at school. Then one day, the sports master, Mr Stewart, moved me to out-half. I honestly don't know why he did, perhaps he just wanted to try me in that position, but I stayed there for the rest of my rugby-playing career. I was very fortunate to be moved to out-half as the position clearly suited my abilities, as I had a quick burst of speed over a short distance."

Jack's secondary schooling was conducted under the shadow of the Second World War. Arrangements to move the school to the north coast were shelved due to parental objections but following the night of 15 April 1941, when Belfast was subjected to a prolonged aerial bombardment by the Luftwaffe, his father moved the family into a B&B in Templepatrick for the rest of the month. He ensured that their schooling did not suffer by driving them all into Belfast first thing in the mornings.

In his final year at B.R.A., Jack was made Head Boy and captain of both the 1st XV and 1st XI. He also made a decision regarding his future career and applied to study medicine at Queen's University, Belfast. These were the days of the Senior Certificate, when students studied a range of subjects rather than the more restrictive A levels. Jack was upset when he failed Latin and Physics but was reassured by his father's reaction *"Well, you gave it a terrible fright and you will definitely get it the next time."* He did his 'resits' during the summer and matriculated in Medicine at QUB in 1944[1].

Jack was in his first year at Queen's when he was called upon to replace Derek Monteith on the 1st XV. Monteith had broken his leg and Jack recalled:

---

1. All medical students at this time had to study Zoology in their first year. They were taught by Professor T. Thompson Flynn who would regale them with stories of his holidays in Hollywood and the Caribbean with his son, the actor Errol Flynn.

Famous Folk from Belfast

"I used to say the cynic might remark that it was a lucky break for me! By the time Derek's leg had healed, Ernie Strathdee and I had established ourselves as half-backs and Derek moved to centre, a position that also suited him and the one in which he played when he captained Ireland in 1947. My rugby career seemed to take off from there really. I was chosen to play for Ulster – I remember a wonderful game against a Kiwi Army side at Ravenhill in November 1945, where Ulster were defeated by the narrowest of margins, 10–9. It was a thrilling match and we came very close to beating them."

In December 1945 Jack, along with another 19 year old Karl Mullen[2], was selected to play for an Irish XV against the British Army at Ravenhill. Internationals had been suspended during the war but this match was a fixture from 1941. Unofficial internationals between the home nations and France started again in 1946, although Caps were not awarded. It was during one of these matches that Jack received his only rugby injury. He collided with a fellow teammate and sustained significant damage to a tendon in his ankle. Fortunately Mr Withers, an Orthopaedic surgeon at the RVH, was in the crowd and sought him out. He arranged for a series of x-rays and put his lower leg in a short-leg cast for two months. While this signalled the end of his rugby season for the year he had reason to be grateful as he was left with no weakness in the joint for the rest of both his rugby career or his later life.

With his leg fully recovered he returned for the 1947 International season and received his first full International Cap on 8th February 1947 against England in Dublin. This was very much the time of the amateur game and such were the restrictions on players that the official notice of selection for the game against Scotland in Murrayfield includes the instruction to *'Please bring one pair clean white knicks'* and *'Players to supply own towels and soap'*. Firmly estab-

---

2. Karl Mullen went on to captain Ireland and was captain of the 1950 British and Irish Lions tour to New Zealand and Australia.

Jack Kyle

lished on the full Irish team he entered the 1948 season quietly confident that the team would perform well. Little did he or his team-mates know that it would be 61 years before an Irish team would equal their performance.

The first match was played on New Year's Day in Paris. It had taken two days to travel by boat and train to Paris, arriving on 30th December. For those of us more familiar with the modern professional game Jack's recollections of their pre-match preparation seem quaint

> *"The international side only got together the day before the match – we didn't meet beforehand for training or talks about tactics – we only had a run-out to exercise our legs for about half an hour in the stadium ... we passed the ball amongst the three-quarters and worked out signals with the scrum-half."*

The night before the match the team were treated to a New Year's Eve outing to the Folies Bergère, although they did return to their hotel before midnight! France 6 – Ireland 13.

The second match was in Twickenham on 14 February against England. Again Kyle scored a try but he also remembers making a mistake when a pass was intercepted by Dickie Guest who scored under the posts. This brought the score to 11-10 and as he later remembered *"I did not enjoy the final ten to fifteen minutes of the game, to put it mildly. I can tell you it was quite a relief to hear the final whistle."* England 10 Ireland 11.

The third match was against Scotland[3] in Landsdowne Road, Dublin. Jack scored an unconverted try [3 points] and Barney Mullen another. Ireland 6 Scotland 0.

---

3. Jack played against Scotland 10 times throughout his International career and was never on the losing side.

Famous Folk from Belfast

The fourth and final match was against Wales and was played at Ravenhill[4] in Belfast. Ireland had not won a Grand Slam since 1899 and *"Wales were a very hard side to play against."* Ireland were the first on the scoreboard with a first half unconverted try by Barney Mullen, but just before the half-time whistle Bleddyn Williams responded for Wales and the teams were level.

> *"In the second half, we broke Welsh hearts early with a try by Jack Daly, our front-row forward ... When Daly was walking back to the halfway line after having score the try, he said 'If Wales don't score again, I'll be canonized!'"*

At the final whistle the score stood at Ireland 6 Wales 3 and the crowd went mad.

> *"I remember the crowd rushing onto the field and carrying off some of the players. Jack Daly had the shirt torn from his back and it was reported that pieces of it were being sold many months later to enthusiastic collectors. We never imagined for one second that it would be sixty-one years before Ireland would win another Grand Slam."*

If Jack Kyle had decided to hang up his rugby boots after this match he would still be remembered as one of the leading players on the team of '48, but he didn't and that decision is the reason why he is still remembered as one of the best rugby players in the world. This is supposed to be an examination of the whole of his life, in a book featuring many more notable individuals and so I am going to have to curb my enthusiasm and select only two more highlights from his rugby career. This is rather difficult as it includes an International career in a green shirt that continued until 1958, 8 appearances for the Barbarians between 1948-54 and

---

4. The Irish team regularly played their 'home' International games at both Ravenhill and Landsdowne Road. The last Five Nations match was played at Ravenhill in February 1954, although the stadium did play host to pool matches in both the 1991 and 1999 Rugby World Cups.

Jack Kyle

6 appearances for the British Lions on their 1950 tour to New Zealand and Australia.

It was the British Lions 1950 tour that cemented his place in Rugby history. Jack was still a medical student at Queen's and his father was less than impressed to read about his selection in the *Belfast Telegraph*, especially as it meant a break of 6 months on the other side of the world. Eric later told Jack that their father had asked *"Does that brother of your ever intend to qualify in medicine?"* Eventually Jack was able to convince his father that he would still be able to continue with his studies onboard SS *Ceramic*, which was taking the team on the four week cruise across the Atlantic, through the Panama Canal and across the Pacific to New Zealand. He and Karl Mullen, who as well as being team captain was studying gynaecology and midwifery, tried to keep each other up to date with their studies.

The tour was a great success with the team winning 22 of the 29 matches and, although they lost the other three test matches, managing to hold the mighty New Zealand All Blacks to a 9 all draw in the first test match. Kyle played in 20 of the matches and so impressed his Kiwi hosts that a local newspaper reported:

> 'Previously, every schoolboy in New Zealand wanted to be a forward, but now they all want to be Jack Kyles.'

Later the same year the *Rugby Almanack of New Zealand* named him as one of their five Players of the year[5] - and called him *'the outstanding genius of the British Isles side.'*

And finally, following a brilliant solo try against France at Ravenhill in 1953 A.P. McWeeney, in the *Irish Independent*, with apologies to the original *Scarlet Pimpernel* penned the following:

---

5. Jack remains one of the few non Kiwis ever to have been awarded this singular honour.

Famous Folk from Belfast

They seek him here, they seek him there
Those Frenchies seek him everywhere.
That paragon of pace and guile,
That damned elusive Jackie Kyle.

Finally, in 1958 and at the age of 32, his international rugby career came to an end. For me the way in which he handled the end says all you need to know about the character of the man. In his authorized biography *Conversations with my Father* by his daughter Justine he recalls:

> "*After one game, Ernie Crawford, who was one of the Irish selectors … came to me and told me that I was to stand up and announce my retirement at a rugby dinner that evening, but I didn't want to do that, it was not my way. I had enjoyed a remarkable rugby career, and I did not mind people knowing I had been dropped from the side. My time was over. I felt it was dishonest to stand up and say I was retiring because everyone knew my days were numbered anyway.*"

As I mentioned earlier, all of this glittering rugby career was being conducted in tandem with his medical studies. He managed to pass all his exams throughout his time at Queens and graduated in 1951 with both his parents in attendance. Having decided to specialize in general surgery he spent a couple of years as a House Surgeon in both the Royal Victoria Hospital and the City Hospital in Belfast before spending a year as Senior House Surgeon working under Jack Balmer in Lurgan, who helped by firing exam-type questions at him and correcting his answers. To help support himself financially he took up a part-time lectureship in the Anatomy Department at Queen's[6]. General Surgery is almost unheard of today when most surgeons specialize in a specific discipline, however

---

6. Both of Jack's parents died within nine months of each other in 1954 and 1955, leaving Jack and Eric responsible for the care of their youngest sister, Beatrice who was still at school at the time. Beatrice was fifteen years younger than Jack.

it could be argued to be one of the more difficult careers within medicine as it requires greater knowledge and a career-long commitment to learning new techniques. To train as such would have been difficult enough for most aspiring surgeons but Jack was undertaking this training while playing representative rugby at the highest level. As he noted himself:

> *"I passed all my exams in my third, fourth and final years at Queen's, despite my six months away with the British and Irish Lions, which I don't think harmed my studies at all."*

In 1959 he was awarded the OBE for services to sport and he passed his final Fellow of the Royal College of Surgeons exam in 1962 and was now able to find a full-time position as a Consultant Surgeon. Inspired, in part, by the life outside Ireland that he had glimpsed on his overseas rugby tours, but also by the desire to *"be seen as a surgeon first and foremost and not as a rugby player who happened to be doing surgery"* he decided to look for positions overseas. He had married Shirley[7], a QUB law graduate, in May 1957 and they were both keen on travelling overseas so he was delighted to be offered a position of consultant surgeon with the Standard Oil Company of New Jersey in Sumatra, Indonesia.

Initially they spent six months in an isolated spot called Pendopo, where there were very few people but there was a man-eating tiger who had killed twenty-seven people. Even here he was pursued by his rugby fame as on a private visit to Hong Kong, when he was recognised by the immigration officer and invited as guest of honour to a function at the Hong Kong rugby club. The next two years were spent in the seventh century capital of southern Sumatra, Palembang where he was slightly busier. One of his clearest memories of this time was when he discovered a young girl of 12 in the

---

7. Sadly, after 10 years Jack's marriage to Shirley ended in divorce. Shirley was bi-polar and the judge awarded full-custody of their two children [Caleb, 6 and Justine, 2] to Jack, although she was given visitation rights.

leper colony. She was frightened as upon the discovery of leprosy in the toes of one foot she had been separated from her family and confined with strangers in the colony. Jack quietly took her to the hospital where he performed a fore-foot amputation on her, which let her return to her family. He treasured the thank you letter she wrote to him.

Civil unrest in the region meant that he decided to return home to Ireland, rather than renew his contract, but he still had itchy feet. A few months after his return he noticed an advert in the BMJ[8] for a consultant surgeon with the Zambia Consolidated Copper mines in Chingola. Little did he know that he was to spend the rest of his working life in the country. The company owned two hospitals in Chingola but when he arrived he was startled to discover that he was the only trained surgeon, not only in Chingola but also in Chililabombwe fifteen miles away. In a country with a population of around 10 million in 1966 there was no medical school and so:

> *"I had to deal with the reality that the country had no neurosurgeons, no vascular surgeons and no plastic surgeons, and there were no obstetricians or gynaecologists in Chingola, so I had to be prepared to turn my hand to any and every type of surgical condition."*

A few years ago Thomas Kane of BBC NI Sports returned to Chingola with Jack, 10 years after his retirement to record a programme *Jack Kyle: A Cut Above*. He reported:

> *"It is hard to describe the welcome Jack received. Everywhere we went in Chingola, people stopped him. Some were old, some were young, some were wealthy, some were from townships. All, though treated Jack with reverence. They were completely in awe of the man who had treated almost everyone in the region."*

The final years Jack spent in Zambia were dominated by the AIDS crisis. The virus first appeared in the early 1980s and doctors were

---

8. British Medical Journal.

baffled by it. By the end of the decade almost 60% of the Zambian population was infected.

> *"I remember on one particular night at the hospital five patients died from AIDS. It was a tragedy unfolding before our eyes. AIDS was the scourge of Africa. Educating the local people was a big problem because they refused to listen to the dangers of sexual promiscuity, though this changed when Kenneth Kaunda's son died of AIDS in 1986. To his great credit, the president did not deny it or try to hide what had happened, but came out and admitted it, which then made it alright for Zambians to talk about it and learn more about it. There was neither the money for the antiviral drugs nor any treatment for those who had contracted the virus and so there was very little we could do for the people, which was incredibly frustrating and sad. I used to talk to the golf caddies and plead with them not to visit prostitutes or to be sexually promiscuous. Sometimes they listened, but there were far too many people who died as a result of the spread of the virus."*

In 1999, after over 30 years in the Chingola, Jack finally decided to retire back to Northern Ireland and bought a house in Byransford, in the shadow of the Mournes. If he had thought that he would slip into obscurity, however, he was mistaken. With the passing of time and the absence of a repeat performance, the significance of the Grand Slam win in 1948 grew greater with every passing season. It seemed to be the impossible dream and the remaining members of the team were cherished by the Irish rugby family. The game moved on from the amateur to the professional era. New stars shone bright and gave us glimpses of genius on the pitch but Jack's stature was not diminished. Even though there were only a few, grainy clips of him on the pitch, his particular genius gathered in status and accolades continued to come his way. Perhaps it was because in the era of professional rugby he had played for the love of the game. However his most cherished award was the Lifetime Achievement award given for his work in Africa by the Irish Journal of Medical Science and the Royal Academy of Medicine in Ireland. In his own mind he was a Surgeon first and foremost.

I have only scratched the surface in this amazing life. I would urge readers who want to learn more to search for the fabulous *Conversations with My Father: Jack Kyle* by his daughter Justine Kyle McGrath, published by Hachette Books Ireland and available as an e-book. Alternatively put his name into an internet search engine and plough through the page after page of articles, videos and photographs.

In a history of what at times is a divisive city it is a rare individual indeed who stands outside the sectarian divide and unites a divided country in unadulterated adoration. Jack Kyle was such an individual. The final word should go to the great man himself in a letter written to Cliff Morgan[9]:

> '*We should try to look on the past with gratitude, on the present with enthusiasm and on the future with confidence.*'

---

9. Welsh rugby player and BBC broadcaster.

John Stewart Bell
1928-1990

Born into a working class family and initially educated at Fane Street Public Elementary before winning a scholarship to the Belfast Technical College, John Bell went on to become one of the 20th century's most respected Physicists. At the time of his untimely death in 1990 he [unknown to him] had been nominated for a Nobel Prize.

I must admit at the start of this chapter that my knowledge of quantum theory is essentially non-existent, so if I make any mistakes in trying to put John Stewart Bell's work into lay language I apologise.

John Stewart Bell was born in Belfast in 1928, the second of four children born to John and Annie Bell. His father had had to leave school aged 12, and both parents placed great emphasis on education.[1] Bell grew up on Tate's Avenue, off the Lisburn Road, and was educated at Fane Street Public Elementary before winning a scholarship to the Belfast Technical College.[2] He was always top of his class and when he was 11 years old announced to his family

---

1. His younger brother David obtained a qualification in electrical engineering from the Belfast Technical College and later became a professor at Lambton College, Canada.
2. The Belfast Technical College was the forerunner of the present day Belfast Metropolitan College.

that he was going to be a scientist and a vegetarian; he never wavered from either decision.

As there was no money for books, the young Bell haunted the library, devouring books on his chosen subject. He finished his schooling at the age of 16 and, too young to start a university course even if his family could have afforded it, found a job as a laboratory assistant in the Physics Department at the Queen's University of Belfast. He so impressed the academic staff, including Professor Karl Emeleus and Dr Robert Sloane, that they gave him books to study and later recommended him for a scholarship to the university.

Their faith in him was not misplaced and he sailed through the course, although at times he clashed with his lecturers as he was trying to advance theories that were beyond current accepted limits. It was during his last two years at Queen's that he started to take formal courses on quantum theory, although his interest had been sparked earlier, by the books he had been lent by Emeleus and Sloane. He graduated with a first class Bachelor of Science degree in experimental physics in 1948 and then, a year later, achieved another first in mathematical physics.

Family circumstances dictated that he had to find a job and as there were no current vacancies at Queens he moved to the Atomic Energy Research Establishment at Harwell, near Oxford. He was assigned to the Theoretical Physics Division, then led by Dr Klaus

John Stewart Bell

Fuchs[3]. He later told a fellow scientist that the only thing that he had noticed was that Dr Fuchs was often absent, no doubt being interviewed about his espionage. Shortly after Dr Fuchs was imprisoned, Bell was approached to join Bill Walkinshaw's[4] accelerator design team at the Telecommunications Research Establishment at Malvern. Walkinshaw later said of John at this time that:

> *'I look back with great pleasure at the sharpness of John's mind and the challenge of keeping up with him. Here was a young man of high caliber who soon showed his independence on choice of project, with a special liking for particle dynamics. His mathematical talent was superb and elegant.*

Also part of the accelerator design team was a talented young mathematics and physics graduate from Glasgow, Mary Ross. In 1954 they were married and she continued her work in accelerator research for the rest of her career.

In 1953 he was granted leave of absence to work in the Department of Mathematical Physics at Birmingham University where he was later to gain a PhD. His work impressed the professor, Rudolf Peierls who remembered that:

---

3. Klaus Emil Julius Fuchs was a Gèrman theoretical physicist who left Germany after the rise of the Nazis, as he was a member of the KPD (Communist party of Germany). Making his home in England, he continued his studies achieving a PhD. Briefly interned at the start of the war, he was approached in 1941 to work on the Tube Alloys programme, the British atomic bomb project, by which time he was already passing research secrets on to the Soviet Union. In 1944 he worked at the Los Alamos Laboratory in America and was present at the Trinity Test in July 1945, before transferring to the Atomic Energy Research Establishment in 1946. He continued to pass on vital research information to the Soviets until his arrest in 1950. He served a nine year prison sentence and upon his release he moved to East Germany and returned to his research. He died on 28 January 1988, a year before the fall of the Berlin Wall.

4. Walkinshaw had worked for the Admiralty during the early years of the war, on the degaussing of submarines, which provides a link between Jack Kyles' father, James Magennis and JS Bell. He later worked on RADAR before moving to the AERE and then Malvern.

Famous Folk from Belfast

'He did not like to take commonly held views for granted but tended to ask 'How do you know?'

Now I have it on good authority[5] that the first part of his doctorial thesis was a proof of the charge conjugation, parity inversion, time reversal (CPT) theorem, while the second part was on functional methods in field theory, but to be honest I have absolutely no idea what any of that means.

While he was still at Harwell he was attached to the Theoretical Physics Division. A colleague, Dr John Perring, said of him at this time that:

'John always stood out through his ability to penetrate to the bottom of any argument and to find the flaws in it by very simple reasoning.'

As part of my research for this chapter I watched several videos, some of them of parts of lectures he had given, and I can attest that he did use simple language to explain his theories, to the extent that I even thought that I understood what he was saying, only to realize later that my O level in Physics was not enough.

At Harwell John's main field of research was nuclear physics. While quantum mechanics was indispensable in his work for accurately calculating the results they needed, the philosophical consideration of the underlying weird reality that the mathematics implied was considered a dead end by many physicists. Indeed a widely used phrase used to those who speculated about what it all meant was *"shut up and calculate"*. Professor Daniel Greenberger, of City College New York, remembered how as a post-graduate student at MIT he had done a lot of reading on the philosophy of quantum mechanics but when he suggested it as a field of study to his supervisor he was warned off.

---

5. An excellent biography of Bell by Philip G. Burke FRS and Ian C Percival FRS published in the Biographical Memoirs Fellows. Royal Society London 45, 1-17 (1999)

John Stewart Bell

In 1960 John and Mary decided that their interest in both elementary particle theory and accelerator design would be better served by moving to CERN in Geneva. John joined the Theory Division and Mary joined the accelerator research group. By the end of their three year contracts they had become permanent members of staff and remained there for the rest of their careers.

CERN, the European Organisation for Nuclear Research, is best known today as being home to the world's largest and most powerful particle accelerator, the Large Hadron Collider. The Theory Division has around ten permanent members of staff, of whom John was one, and up to a hundred visiting scientists. His colleagues always comment upon his 'honesty' and 'generosity' and what is meant by this is probably best described by Burke and Percival who observed that:

> *'Even when confronted with an immediate practical problem, he was always concerned with matters of principle. He was never one to work on a problem without obtaining a full understanding of both the problem and its origins. This led to advances in fields that others considered closed. Once he was sure that the physics was understood, he tended to lose interest. His collaborators often continued for many years along lines of research that they had started with him.'*

However, unlike many in his position, he was happy for them to take the credit for the original idea when they published the work. In a video available online, *Action at a distance: The life and legacy of John Stewart Bell*, some of the leading names in Physics, such as Reinhold Bertlmann of Vienna, Prof Dr. Anton Zeilinger and John Clauser all keep returning to the theme of his honesty and generosity. Professor Andrew Whitaker of the Department of Physics at QUB said that:

> *'Once established he was generous in promoting younger scientists – he would think of an idea then pass it on for them to develop so that they could get the credit and promote their careers.'*

Famous Folk from Belfast

In CERN his main area of research was in nuclear physics, ironically he considered his interest in the foundations and philosophy behind quantum mechanics as his hobby. He was often heard to comment that:

> '*I work on a daily basis on certain problems, but on Sundays I have principles.*'

It was this hobby that was to settle a major disputes in the world of quantum physics and throw some light on the underlying reality of the world we live in.

Mathematical physics used to be known as Natural Philosophy and much of it was indeed philosophical. In the 1920s and 30s there was an on going philosophical dispute between the two great figures of 20th century physics, Einstein and Bohr, about the fundamental nature of reality. At the atomic scale, quantum theory says that any given particle can exist in different states or even places all at the same time and all that you could say about it was how probable it would be that if you looked for it in a particular place or state you would find it there. Only when a measurement is taken, does the particle adopt a particular state.

Essentially Bohr thought that this weird interpretation of reality that emerged from the mathematics of quantum theory was a true reflection of what was actually happening whereas Einstein thought that such weirdness was only an illusion caused by our lack of knowledge of deeper underlying processes famously saying "[God] does not play dice with the universe".

Another weird consequence of quantum mechanics is that of 'entanglement' when two particles become intimately connected. Once such entanglement occurs the particles can be moved apart but still seem to be connected in some way in that observing some property of one of the particles results in an <u>instantaneous</u> effect

John Stewart Bell

for the other which seemed to violate Einstein's theory of relativity.

Einstein believed that this instantaneous change could not be due to some sort of a connection between the particles (which he described as 'spooky action at a distance') but rather the instantaneous changes, which had been observed, were caused by hidden information carried by the particles from the moment they became entangled.

Whether Einstein was correct or not was to remain a philosophical argument for many years as no one had any idea as to how the debate could be settled. That was until, in 1964, John Bell published a paper entitled *On the Einstein-Podolsky-Rosen Paradox* which included a mathematical formula which became known as Bell's Theorem. This theorem opened the way to experimentally test whether Einstein's 'hidden information' or Bohr's 'spooky action at a distance' was correct.

Although Bell developed his theory in 1964, experimental technology took several years to catch up and it was not until 1982 when a team of scientists in Paris were able to set up an experiment to get the necessary data to check what results Bells theorem produced. Their results unequivocally showed that in this instance Einstein had been wrong and that 'spooky action at a distance' did exist.

Prof Andrew Whitaker of Queens states that Bell's work opened the door to the possibility of the future development of quantum information theory, quantum computation, quantum cryptography and quantum teleportation – huge areas of research, far beyond its original scope. Daniel Greenberger said that the paper came out of the blue and woke the scientific community up from a thirty year nap.

While John Bell is best known for his 'hobby' of quantum physics, his proper job remained research into high energy physics, to which he also added accelerator dynamics. In the early 1980s he collaborated with Mary in the study of electron cooling in storage rings for the antiproton accumulator machine. Later they collaborated together on a *'detailed practical study of 'quantum beamstrahlung'.*[6]

John died at his home in Geneva from a cerebral haemorrhage on 1 October 1990, unaware that he had been nominated for a Nobel prize. The first recipient of the John Stewart Bell Prize, Nicholas Gisin said of him:

> *John Bell was an absolute master. There is no shadow of doubt that he sits next to the giants such as Newton, Maxwell and Einstein*

I genuinely would have loved to have been in a position to explain his work in more detail, however it was in the realms of genius. It is natural to compare him to our other famous mathematical physicist, William, Lord Kelvin. However, I feel that Bell was perhaps greater than Kelvin. Kelvin was born into an academic family and was able to start attending his father's university lectures at the age of 10. John, however, had to fight to find his way to an academic education. His parents couldn't afford to send him to a grammar school, he wasn't even entered into any of the available scholarships. At the Belfast Technical College, he originally studied brick laying. And still he found a way to access the world he had dreamt about as an eleven year old boy in Tate's Avenue. He still found a way to prove that Einstein was wrong.

> *We have to take the world as it is given to us and live with it.*
>
> *John Stewart Bell.*

---

6. Burke and Percival

Henry Joy and Mary Ann McCracken
1767-1798   1770-1866
United Irishman & Social reformer

The charismatic leader of the United Irishmen in the north of Ireland, McCracken was hanged for his part in the rebellion. His sister and life long confidant, Mary Ann, fully supported him, taking in his illegitimate daughter after his death and raising her as her own. Mary Ann was an extremely active social reformer right up to her death at age 96.

Most people will have heard about Henry John McCracken, the tall handsome United Irishmen leader who was hanged close to his family's Belfast home[1]. Fewer people will have heard about his sister Mary Ann, who held his hand as he walked to the gallows and who is usually last seen weeping over his body. So long as he was alive, the story of Henry Joy, or Harry as the family called him, was closely intertwined with that of his younger sister and closest confidant. However, she was only twenty-seven when he died and lived until she was ninety-six. We think of her as an eighteenth century personality, but sixty-six years of her life was lived in the nineteenth century, and for all of those years she was actively involved in the life of her hometown.

---

1. His maternal great-grandfather Martin had donated the land on the site of the present-day Cornmarket, to the people of Belfast to build a Market House.

Famous Folk from Belfast

Mary Ann and Harry[2] were children of Captain John and Ann McCracken and were brought up in a house on High Street. Through their mother they were related to one of the leading families in Belfast – the Joys – and their Joy relations lived close by. As well as owning the *Belfast News Letter*[3], the Joys also owned cotton mills and, unusually for an eighteenth century woman, their mother owned a small muslin business.

As newspaper proprietors the Joy family were abreast of all the latest, radical ideas of the Enlightenment about politics, philosophy, religion and education. They were followers of the 'New Light' form of Presbyterianism, which placed great emphasis on reading the Bible, as a means of coming to a personal relationship with God, and service to the poor. The young Mary Ann and her older sister Margaret helped to sew clothes for the inmates of the Belfast Charitable Society's Poorhouse, which had been set up earlier by concerned citizens, including her own relations. It was an early introduction to the harsh realities of life in a rapidly expanding town.

The McCracken and Joy children were sent to be educated at David Manson's school, which was heavily influenced by the new ideas on education promoted by Enlightenment figures such as Jean-Jacques Rousseau who stated that *'the noblest work in education is to make a reasoning man.'* Manson was unusual as not only did he resist the temptation to resort to corporal punishment to control his pupils, but he also provided the same education to the girls in his charge as to the boys.

---

2. I will be calling H J McCracken 'Harry' throughout as there are a lot of Henrys in this story, a couple of whom are called Henry Joy, and it gets confusing.

3. Ann McCracken's father Francis Joy was a lawyer but, as a result of bad debt, he acquired a small printing press in 1737 and set up the *New Letter*. He later set up the first cotton mill in Belfast and imported the first Spinning Jenny.

Henry Joy and Mary Ann McCracken

The McCracken household also included their paternal grandmother, a redoubtable old lady who

> *'in protest against the iniquity of set-days and holy-days would sit ostentatiously in the window on a Christmas Day busily engaged at the spinning wheel.*[4]

Another member of the household was a young apprentice organist from St Anne's church, called Edward 'Atty' Bunting. He was to remain with the family until his marriage in his thirties. He is best known today as the 'father' of Irish Traditional music. He spent many years travelling around Ireland collecting and transposing traditional harp music[5]. Patrick Lynch, who wrote down the Irish lyrics to the airs, often accompanied him. Captain McCracken was keen that all his children should be able to speak another language and employed an old French weaver to teach them French.

While Harry and Mary Ann were still at school, Belfast was set alight by the news of the American colonists' Declaration of Independence. This was of especial interest to the Presbyterians in Belfast as, apart from close trading links many of their relations had emigrated to the American colonies to escape famine, poverty and political restrictions in Ireland. Presbyterians were subject to the Test Act[6], the same as Catholics and other petty restrictions, such as not recognizing their marriages and of course the detested Tithe, so many of the complaints of the revolting Americans would have struck a chord with their Belfast kinsmen and women.

---

4. McNeill, Mary, *The life and times of Mary Ann McCracken*. Allen Figgis & Co, Dublin, 1960.

5. Bunting published the music, transposed for piano, in three volumes of *The Ancient Music of Ireland*.

6. This was actually a series of Test Acts that were applied to Roman Catholics and non-conformists. Only people who could prove that they were members of the Anglican church [Church of Ireland] were eligible for public office and commissions in the navy or army.

Famous Folk from Belfast

The support for the rebels was tempered when Paul Jones, an American privateer, sailed his boat *Ranger* into Belfast Lough and fired on Carrickfergus. The whole of Ireland had been stripped of soldiers and the merchants of Belfast organized a militia[7], calling themselves Irish Volunteers, originally to defend themselves. The Belfast Volunteers invited *'persons of every religious persuasion'* to join their ranks. The idea quickly spread and soon there were Irish Volunteers throughout Ireland. As the threat from America receded the movement started to demand greater political and economic freedom from Westminster[8] for the Irish parliament and saw a limited degree of success with what is known as Grattan's Parliament. One of their main political demands was for Catholic emancipation and the repeal of the Penal laws, which placed restrictions of Roman Catholics and Presbyterians alike.

Their Joy family and neighbours in High Street were all members of the Belfast Volunteers and conversations around the dinner table and at parties were about the latest 'radical' ideas of political and economic liberalism.

In *Belfast*, Bill Maguire says that once the threat of invasion had receded *the Volunteer corps became middle-class political clubs* which held parades, dinners and balls. In the main they were 'radical' or liberal in outlook and held on to the original demands for emancipation. When St. Mary's, the first Roman Catholic Church in Belfast, was built in 1784, the Belfast Volunteers (including the Joy uncles) paraded and attended the first church service[9]. With such an upbringing it should not come as a surprise to learn that both

---

7. Due to the lack of soldiers the authorities were happy to turn a blind eye to this flouting of the Test Act.

8. Not to be confused with the Home Rule agitation of the next century, this was before the Act of Union.

9. Most of the money for the construction of St Mary's was raised by the town's Presbyterian merchants, as while there were some middle-class Catholic merchants most of Belfast's Catholics were too poor to meet the cost.

Henry Joy and Mary Ann McCracken

young McCrackens showed an interest in radicalism themselves as they approached maturity.

As their education came to an end Harry and Mary Ann began to think about their future. As was usual for a son of merchant family, Harry was apprenticed to a family cotton mill. Rather usually Mary Ann and her older sister Margaret set up a muslin embroidery business. They commissioned muslin from hand-loom weavers and then employed girls and women to do the embroidery in the McCracken family home[10]. Their other siblings were also established in the family businesses. Their eldest brother Francis [an early recruit for both the Volunteers and the United Irishmen] ran their father's rope works and sailcloth factory. William, who was also prominent in the United Irishmen, was employed in the cotton industry and the baby of the family, John, who avoided political involvement, became one of the leading cotton manufacturers in the town.

Harry displayed his social conscious while still a young man. Together with several other concerned citizens he open the first Sunday School in Belfast to teach poor men and women to read and write. While this would improve their employment and social circumstances it was motivated by the Presbyterian dedication to reading the Bible as a route to spiritual salvation. Margaret and Mary Ann's muslin embroidery business, although efficiently run was seen as an extension of her charitable work by providing employment to hand-loom weavers (already beginning to be squeezed out of employment by the increasing number of factories) and girls and women from the Poorhouse.

The news of the French Revolution in 1789 was, according to their cousin (and now proprietor of the *Belfast News Letter*) Henry Joy

---

10. The McCrackens had moved from High Street to Rosemary Lane, close to their church.

jnr, met with exultation by the people of Belfast, many of whom had French Huguenot ancestry. The support continued for some time as the Volunteers organized celebrations the following year on the anniversary of the fall of the Bastille. In 1790 a Whig Club was started in Belfast with Henry Joy jnr one of the first members. So many people read Thomas Paine's *The Rights of Man* when it was published in 1791 that Wolfe Tone described it as *'The Koran of Belfeseu.'*

Around the same time that *The Rights of Man* was circulating, so too were a series of pamphlets by a young Dublin barrister called Theobald Wolfe Tone, who was secretary of the Catholic Committee in Dublin. One of his best friends was a handsome young officer in the 64th Regiment of Foot, Thomas Russell, who in 1791 was set with his regiment to Belfast. Russell was very interested in music and sought out Bunting, who in turn brought him home to meet the McCrackens. Both Harry and Mary Ann enjoyed the company of Russell for slightly different reasons. They both enjoyed debating politics with him, however Mary Ann's interest was slightly more personal. Many years later she described him to Dr Madden [11] as:

> *'A model of manly beauty, he was one of those favoured individuals who one cannot pass in the street without being guilty of staring in the face while passing and turning round to look at the receding figure... the benevolence that beamed in his fine countenance seemed to mark him out as one, who was destined to be the ornament, grace and blessing of private life.'*

Harry and Russell joined in discussions with others of like mind in Belfast who were impatient for political reform and with Wolfe Tone they resolved to form a Society of United Irishmen, which harked back to the original declaration of the Belfast Volunteers

---

11. R R Madden was a nineteenth century historian of the United Irishmen. Mary Ann co-operated fully with him and maintained a correspondence with him for many years.

in appealing for a union of religious faiths in Ireland *'to abolish the differences that had long divided Irishmen.'*

There is some confusion as to whether or not Harry was actually in the inaugural meeting of the United Irishmen but he was certainly privy to all the discussions leading up to it and was very active thereafter. Given the closeness between brother and sister, Mary Ann would also have been fully aware of and sympathetic to their aims. Both Francis and William McCracken also joined the Society.

We often think of the United Irishmen as a secret organization, and certainly after 1794 it was, however in the early years it was perfectly legal and open in both membership and objectives. It even had its own newspaper, *The Northern Star*, which was published in Belfast by Samuel Neilson and, despite their connections, was very popular in the McCracken household. Mary Ann's niece later recalled;

> *"The ladies of the family took a lively, if less active interest in politics. The Northern Star was attentively perused. Miss Mary once exclaimed, on recovering from a fever – "Oh I have missed so many of the Star".'*

The new organization appealed to the younger generation in Belfast and further afield who viewed the Volunteers as somewhat old fashioned and with young, handsome and charismatic leaders such as Harry and Wolfe Tone, touring Ireland their ranks rapidly increased. It was particularly popular amongst the rural workers of counties Down and Antrim, where a Presbyterian majority meant that they were less likely to fear their Catholic neighbours (if in fact they had any) but where the disadvantages of religious restrictions, absentee landlords and short land leases created a natural disaffection with the *status quo*.

Famous Folk from Belfast

Nor was membership restricted solely to men, as there were a few Ladies Societies[12] and Martha McTier (sister of Dr William Drennan) mentions *'a meeting of our select society'* in a letter. However, while she knew of their existence Mary Ann was not a member and in a letter to Harry as late as 16 March 1797 she expressed grave doubts as to their purpose other than:

> *'keeping the women in the dark ... to make tools of [them] without confiding in them.'*

She continued:

> *'I wish to know if they have any rational ideas of liberty and equality for themselves or whether they are contented with their present abject and dependent situation, degraded by custom and education beneath the rank in society in which they were originally placed.'*

There was no reason to suppose that the Society was going to be any different from the Volunteers, and that while they were agitating for political reform they would plan for open revolt. They were tolerated by the authorities in Dublin, and so things might have continued had the French not declared war on Britain in 1793. The administration became alarmed at the pro-French sympathies of the Society and it was banned in 1794. The authorities started to operate a carrot and stick approach to the government of Ireland, with the removal of many of the restrictions of Catholics up to but not including the vote culminating with the founding of St Patrick's seminary at Maynooth in 1795, while at the same time suspending *habeas corpus*, raising a yeomanry to suppress any insurrection and search for arms, and the arrest of the known United Irishmen leaders including William and Harry and Thomas Russell.

Mary Ann's letters to Harry while he was confined in Kilmainham jail in Dublin provide a great insight into the relationship between

---

12. The Ladies Societies were kept separate from the main Society and their purpose was to provide support.

Henry Joy and Mary Ann McCracken

the siblings as well as life in late eighteenth century Ireland. Harry was arrested on 10 October 1796 and as Mary McNeill says

> *'from now onwards every stage in the bitter tragedy was share by Mary Ann, every step taken on Harry's behalf was directed by her.'*

Mary Ann, using the excuse of her muslin business was able to make several visits to see him in captivity. A Joy cousin, Henry Joy[13], was a lawyer in Dublin so she had a place to stay in Temple Street. As their confinement continued Mary Ann used the income from her muslin business and actual gifts of muslin to Mrs Richardson, his jailor's wife, to try to alleviate their conditions. Harry was able to join a circulating library and to take some exercise as well as receiving and sending letters. However the damp conditions did nothing to improve his health and he began to complain of rheumatism. He was joined by other Belfast United Irishmen, including his brother William and a few months later William's wife Rose Ann was allowed to join them, although she was not arrested.

Informers infiltrated what was left of the United Irishmen in Belfast and throughout the country. In a letter to *'dear Harry'* on 18 April 1797 Mary Ann tell of the search of several houses:

> *'it is supposed Newell the painter was the informer [as] they were conducted by a little man dressed as a cavalry officer with a handerchief tied across his mouth who everyone of the family instantly recognised.'*

The authorities had a prison ship at anchor in the Belfast Lough and Mary Ann watched as prisoners were marched to the docks.

By the time that William and Harry were released on bail in December 1797 most of the leadership was either in exile [Wolfe Tone], or prison, [Russell et al], and the Northern Star had been suppressed. The authorities had used a mixture of political conces-

---

13. Now do you see why I am using 'Harry"?

Famous Folk from Belfast

sions and military might to great effect and were confident that the threat of rebellion was receding. Despite their optimism what was left of the United Irishmen leadership were, however, determined to proceed. Under cover of selling his mother's fabrics Harry travelled to Dublin to try to help the prisoners and liaise with Lord Edward Fitzgerald[14], the leader in Leinster. On 12 May 1798 he wrote to Mary Ann from Dublin asking after his father's health, giving information about business transactions and then commenting that:

> 'there are most horrid accounts from the county Kildare you must certainly have heard some of them, but I suppose the worst you have heard is nothing in comparison to the real state of that unfortunate county'.

The leaders still hoped that Wolfe Tone would secure French help but in its absence they decided to go ahead on 23 May. When Samuel Neilson and Lord Edward were arrested it was postponed, but only by a couple of weeks. On 5 June Sir Edward Crosbie[15] of Carlow was executed for treason following a pre-emptive rising in the town. Harry was made leader in the North and, ordering them to attack military posts in their neighbourhoods, issued a proclamation on 6 June 1798:

> '*Tomorrow we march on Antrim – drive the garrison of Randalstown before you and hasten to form a junction with the Commander-in-chief Henry Joy McCracken. The First Year of Liberty.*'

---

14. Lord Edward Fitzgerald was a son of the Duke of Leinster. Through his mother he was first cousin to Charles James Fox the great Whig MP, and was also a descendant of Charles II.

15. Sir Edward Crosbie of Viewmount House, Carlow was hanged and then his head was displayed on a pike in Carlow. The court martial rejected his defence of mistaken identity. Sir Edward's brother Richard was the first Irishman to make a manned flight after flying in a hydrogen air balloon from Ranelagh to Clontarf on 19 January 1785. They share a common ancestor with the author.

Henry Joy and Mary Ann McCracken

The attacks went forward but they had been betrayed to General Nugent and despite risings in Antrim and Co. Down in the North the rebellion was crushed. I do not propose to go into a blow for blow account of the battles. If you are really interested then please read *Summer Soldiers* by the late, great A.T.Q. Stewart.

Harry was joined at Antrim by William and William's brother-in-law James McGlathery, so one can imagine the tension in the McCracken home in Rosemary Lane as they waited for news. When it was all over the rebels were dead, arrested or, in the case of the McCracken brothers, in hiding. Belfast was under curfew and the countryside under martial law, as General Nugent threatened to burn towns, villages and farms if there was not an immediate surrender of arms.

After a week without news Mary Ann and Rose Ann set out on foot to search for their loved ones. They found Rose Ann's brother James in a gardener's cottage near Whitehouse and learnt from him that William was safe and hiding at a relative's house. They were told that Harry was somewhere in the hills overlooking Belfast, and after several hours of search they found him with six companions.

Having assured themselves that Harry was uninjured the women returned home, but lines of communication had been set up. It seems amazing to us today, given that the countryside was full of militia and informers, but Harry and Mary Ann were able to exchange letters and she was able to provide him with money and provisions. Mary worked hard to secure a forged pass for Harry and arranged with one of their father's friends *'who was captain of a foreign ship'* to take Harry to America, but before he could make his escape he was recognised and taken prisoner.

He was held for a couple of days in Carrickfergus jail and then on 16 July he was transferred to Belfast and held in the barracks on

Famous Folk from Belfast

Ann Street, before his court martial the following day. Mary Ann was present for the trial and forty years later she told Dr Madden:

> 'The moment I set my eyes upon him I was struck with the extraordinary serenity and composure of his look. This was no time to think about such things but yet I could not help gazing on him, it seemed to me that I had never seen him look so well, so full of healthful bloom, so free from the slightest trace of care or trouble, as at that moment when he was perfectly aware of his approaching fate.'

The outcome was a foregone conclusion. He was returned to the barracks and Mary Ann was with him when Major Fox:

> 'came to the door of my brother's cell ... and I heard him say, "You are ordered for immediate execution". My poor brother seemed to be astonished at the announcement, indeed he well might be at the shortness of the time allotted to him;"

She continued that she:

> 'felt a strange sort of composure and self-possession ... I knew that it was incumbent on me to avoid disturbing the last moments of my brother's life.'

He asked to see the family minister, but Rev Steel Dickson who was also a prisoner at the barracks arrived first and upon seeing him *burst into tears, exclaiming "Oh Harry, you did not know how much I loved you."'* Mary Ann and Harry drew comfort from their faith and '*the firm conviction of an all-wise and overruling Providence and of the duty of entire resignation to the Divine Will.*'

At 5pm Mary Ann accompanied him to the gallows, but at his request left him before the end. Unlike others, such as Sir Edward Crosbie, Harry was not decapitated after hanging and his body was returned to the family. Mary Ann had arranged with a family friend, Dr McDonnell, to attempt to revive him, but to no avail. Accompanied by their younger brother John and a handful of friends, Mary Ann took her brother's corpse to the Parish burial ground for her final goodbye.

On her last visit to her brother Mary Ann later remembered that she had asked him if there was anything else that he wanted her to do for him.

> '"No", he replied, hesitatingly, but from his look I judged there was something occupying his thoughts which he did not wish to mention. What was then stirring in his mind flashed on mine like lightning ... and the source of his anxiety became a source of comfort to me and a means of fulfilling a duty to his memory.'

This source of comfort was a little girl, called Maria[16] who it appears Harry had fathered out of wedlock, although no one was in any doubt about her paternity, as she was blessed with her father's good looks. In the face of considerable opposition within the family and scandal in Belfast society, Mary Ann took the child into the family home and raised her as her own daughter.

Not only had Mary Ann lost her beloved Harry but also to add to her grief her brothers Francis and William were also wanted men. Francis made plans to go to America, which were later cancelled, but William was arrested. Mary Ann gained an interview with General Lake and managed to persuade him to release William on bail.

At least she knew that Russell was safe. He was still in Newgate prison in Dublin, so had been unable to take part in the rebellion. The next year he was moved to Fort George in Scotland and was then sent into exile on the continent. He had asked Mary Ann to try to support his sister Margaret, who was living in Dublin, and she regularly sent what she could afford and would often ask their friends for donations. In 1803 Russell returned to live with a

---

16. It is supposed that Maria's mother was Mary Bodel, in whose father's cottage Harry had hidden after the revolt.

weaver, who worked for Mary, on the outskirts of Belfast. He had become involved with Robert Emmett and together they had been laying plans for another revolt.

However, there was little appetite for further rebellion in Belfast and on 15 July Russell wrote to Francis to tell him that he had decided to leave and so it came as a surprise to the family when they learnt that the rebellion had gone ahead with predictable results. Once again Mary Ann was actively involved in trying to help a fugitive to escape from the authorities. She paid two fishermen in Bangor to take him to Drogheda. The plan was that he would then try to escape to the continent, but he was arrested on 9 September. On 21 October he was hanged and then decapitated in Downpatrick.

The Act of Union was passed and Mary Ann now had a small girl to educate and care for. She and Margaret continued to expand their embroidered muslin business and employed two agents in Dublin. They were pioneers in the production of patterned and checked muslin and so popular were their patterns that they could hardly keep up with the demand. Unfortunately, after advancing loans to bad creditors, the sisters had to close their business in 1815.

While she no longer had a business of her own, Mary Ann was able to devote herself to trying to alleviate the living and working conditions of the poor in her hometown. Belfast was growing at a great rate but the living and working conditions were not keeping up with the growth. Periodic famines and economic downturns put great pressure on the Belfast Charitable Society. Mary Ann served as secretary on the 'Ladies Committee' for over twenty years, and tirelessly lobbied the 'Gentlemen's Committee', who controlled the purse strings, to reform and improve conditions. It was her idea to set up a nursery at the Poor House to provide the children with a basic education. She also requested that the children should be given candles and books so that they could read for pleasure, enjoy a better diet, have access to toys and outdoor exercise and have access to clean water and soap.

Nor were her efforts solely confined to their material benefit. She insisted that children should be found apprenticeships, but that they should be supervised by the Charitable Society and allowed to return if the person to whom they had been apprenticed proved unreliable or cruel. She often took it upon herself to visit to check on conditions herself. In fact it could be argued that more care was taken over their charges than many young men and women who had not grown up at the Poor House and who were frequently used as slave labour or abused by their employers

For the rest of the nineteenth century there was scarcely a 'radical' cause that she did not support. She campaigned to outlaw the use of boy chimney sweeps, to improve women's employment conditions, prison reform and against the slave trade. So passionate was she about the abolition of the slave trade in America that she gave up sugar, despite having a very sweet tooth, and aged 89 was standing on the docks handing out leaflets denouncing the slave plantations of the southern states, to emigrants boarding the ships.

She was a fierce defender of her beloved Harry's memory and collected as many of his letters as she could. In 1840 Dr Madden asked her to help him with a book about the United Irishmen and we can hear her voice, loud and clear, in its pages. She was a committed Christian and thought it her duty to help those less fortunate than herself. She remained a much-loved member of her extended family, with whom she lived until her final days. During the research for this chapter I discovered that when she was the model for the old gypsy lady in Nicholas Joseph Crowley's *Fortune Telling By Cup Tossing* a lovely portrait of one of the great ladies of Belfast.

She lived out the last years of her life with her adopted daughter Maria and her family. She was a little deaf, a little blind and suffering from rheumatism, but her passion for life and reform were undiminished until the end. She was in her nineties and had seen great change in the world at large and her own home. In one letter she mentions the *'discoveries in nature, inventions in art, almost like magic.'* She had even had her photograph taken. Her niece Anna McCleery recorded the end of this remarkable life:

> *'She faded peacefully and gently away, apparently contented and happy, without weariness or pain, until, after some hours of unconsciousness she breathed her last.'*

She was 96 years old. She was buried within the shadow of the Poorhouse, she had spent most of her life supporting.

I am going to finish with two quotes, both from Mary Ann which I feel sum up her life, both were written to Dr Madden, almost half a century after 1798:

> *'Notwithstanding the grief that overcomes every feeling for a time and still lingers in my breast ... I never once wished that my beloved brother had taken any other part than that which he did take.*
>
> *This world affords no enjoyment equal to that of promoting the happiness of others, it so far surpasses mere selfish gratification from its not only being pleasant at the time but from affording agreeable recollections afterwards.'*

JAMES ELLIS
1931-2014

Actor, director, poet, author

Best known for his long running role as PC Bert Lynch on the TV series Z Cars, Ellis, with his strong Ulster accent was one of the leading lights in the UK entertainment scene.

Despite recent polls, always pointed out to me by my beloved husband, that the Northern Irish accent is now considered to be one of the most 'sexy' it is still relatively rarely heard on our airwaves. Adrian Dunbar and Stephen Kennedy [Ian Craig on The Archers] are notable exceptions, as many of our homegrown actors prove very adept at adopting other accents. While the accent is still rare, in the 1960s it was almost unheard, outside news reports. Flying the flag, however, was one man whose dulcet Belfast tones could be heard twice a week on the most successful police drama across the two available T.V. channels. The character of PC Bert Lynch appeared in 629 episodes of the long running drama and he was played by one of Belfast's own, James Ellis.

James Ellis was born in east Belfast in March 1931, almost within sight of the gantries of the Harland and Wolffe shipyard where his father, uncle and many male relations, past and present, were employed. He was born at a time of great economic unrest in his home city, with mass unemployment, the Outdoor Relief Strike etc. and his father had to move the family over to England in search of employment. However, after a short time they returned to Belfast and eventually took up residence in the house in Park Avenue that was to remain in the family until the turn of this century. The proximity of the family home to the shipyard meant that they were at great risk during the Belfast Blitz of 1941 and Jimmy later recalled his father carrying an unexploded incendiary device from their home.

He enjoyed a happy, secure childhood in a loving family, although money was not overly plentiful. His parents were both very proud when he was one of 100 boys to win a City Scholarship and gained a place at Methodist College, Belfast. Unlike nowadays when most children are expected to stay in school until 18, admission to the sixth form (and therefore University) was strictly controlled. Jimmy had performed quite well in his Junior exams but still had to *'literally talk myself into the exclusive sixth form in an interview with the amiable but exacting vice-principal 'Pop' Rose.'* Most of his year won places at Oxbridge or Trinity College Dublin, but he and another friend, James Greene, won scholarships to the Queen's University, Belfast.

He had taken part in various school dramatic performances but it was while at Queen's that he really caught the acting bug and both he and James joined the Dramatic Society. In an attempt to earn some much needed money they started appearing in the Arts Theatre on Fountain Street. While James Greene was to go on to finish his degree, Jimmy's life was to take a different course. He won the prestigious Tyrone Guthrie[1] Scholarship

---

1. Sir William Tyrone Guthrie was one of the leading theatrical directors of the twentieth century. He was a great supporter of local theatre, throughout Ireland, although his reputation as a director was international.

James Ellis

> *'which was a carefully thought out scheme to attend the Bristol Old Vic school, work backstage at every aspect of stage management, attend rehearsals of particular productions ... and direct a play of my own choosing using my fellow students, at Bristol University. I chose T.S. Eliot's **The Cocktail Party** with my cast featuring Phyllida Law, the mother-to-be of Emma Thompson'*

Upon completion of his scholarship Tyrone Guthrie arranged a job for him in a touring production of *The Glass Menagerie* with the salary of £11 per week, a rate of pay that he discovered was only payable for touring. After this tour he joined the Ulster Group Theatre, under the directorship of Harold Goldblatt, on a weekly salary of £3. The Group Company was home to a range of outstanding actors, several of whom went on to have glittering careers on stage and screen outside their hometown. Two of the most prominent were Colin Blakely and Billy Millar, who changed his name to Stephen Boyd and starred in Hollywood films including *Ben Hur*. Jimmy always credited his time at the Group with teaching him his trade, with older actors such as the wonderful J. G. Devlin helping to train the youngsters.

His experience in the Bristol Old Vic gave him the confidence to put himself forward as a director as well as an actor and within a relatively short time he had become artistic director, while still in his mid-twenties. One summer he was 'lent' to Marjory Mason, who was running a small repertory company in Bangor to replace their leading actor who had become ill. He ended up staying with the company for the rest of the season and even took over the role of director when Marjory decided to go to England. It was then that he started up his relationship with the actress who was to become his first wife, Betty Hogg, who was a member of the company. His old school friend James Greene was also a member of the cast, and soon the company was attracting an audience from outside the seaside resort, as people travelled down from Belfast to the Little Theatre.

Famous Folk from Belfast

He had now shown that he was able to turn his hand to all aspects of the theatre, as well as being a very promising young actor. As the summer season came to an end he was approached by Joseph Tomelty (father of actresses Frances and Roma) to direct his latest play, *To Have a Little House*, which marked his return to the stage after a traumatic car crash had left him in a coma for eleven weeks. Unfortunately, it soon became apparent that Joseph was suffering from memory loss and the play closed quite quickly. Jimmy, however, was in great demand and was offered the job of Assistant Artistic Director of the Group Theatre.

As Assistant Artistic Director he was determined to stamp his authority and vision on the company, although he privately quailed at giving artistic direction to actors old enough to be his father. Off stage he was anxious that the Group Theatre Company should build on the success he had had in Bangor the previous summer. The summer months were traditionally lean ones for the Group as their audience left the city on holiday. Jimmy argued that they could simply move down to the Little Theatre, and so increase their profits. The idea was a great success and so he might have continued, a talented young actor/director in Belfast, if he hadn't been asked to read the script for a play in 1959.

The author was a man from a very similar background called Sam Thompson and the play was called *Over the Bridge*.

Like Jimmy, Sam Thompson came from a protestant working class background. Unlike Jimmy, he had left school at 14 to start work as a painter in Harland and Wolffe. He had become a committed trade unionist and, after the Second World War, had been a shop steward when working for the Belfast Corporation. His militancy cost him his job with the Corporation, but a chance meeting with

James Ellis

Sam Hanna Bell[2] in a pub lead to a new career, in his early 40s, writing plays for BBC Northern Ireland. When he approached Jimmy with his script about life in the shipyard he said *"I've got a play you won't touch with a bargepole."* Jimmy glanced at the script and took it home for his father to read. In his autobiography Jimmy recalled that

> *'I took it back to my parents hoping my father, himself a shipyard worker, would cast his eye over the script. Not only did he do that but he sat poring over the entire play, re-reading many passages. When he had finished, at well past midnight, he handed it back and said 'This is our play son, you must do it.'*

So what was the play and why was it so controversial? It is set in the shipyard and concerns a sectarian dispute between two workers, one protestant, Archie Kerr, the other catholic, Peter O'Boyle. A Trade Union official, Davy Mitchell, calls both parties in to try to sort out the dispute but it only exacerbates the situation with each making serious allegations about the other. Later there is an explosion at the shipyard, which some claim to have been caused by an IRA bomb and an angry mob order all Catholics to leave the yard. The next day only one catholic worker shows up for work, Peter O'Boyle. A mob comes looking for O'Boyle but Davy manages to get him to the foreman's office while the foreman tries to phone for the police. The phone lines have been cut so Davy goes out to try to reason with the mob. He comes back saying that if O'Boyle leaves the shipyard by lunchtime then no harm will come to him. O'Boyle refuses saying that it is Davy's job as a Trade Unionist to protect his right to work. Faced with this Davy decides to accompany O'Boyle back to his work. As they walk through the mob it falls silent, then there is a rushed attack and Davy is killed, while

---

2. Sam Hanna Bell was novelist, playwright and producer with the BBC Northern Ireland. He is most famous for his novel December Bride which was made into a film starring Saskia Reeves and Ciaran Hinds in 1991.

O'Boyle is seriously injured. The final scene is the next day when some of the union officials are arguing over what has happened. One of them, Warren Baxter who had witnessed the attack from his office window says

> '*A man told me yesterday, that when the mob went into action he walked away, and so did hundreds of his so-called respectable workmates because they said it was none of their business ... and that's what frightens me ... they walked away.*'

Since the end of the war, Belfast had been relatively peaceful, depending on your viewpoint. And people at the top of society, who were in positions of power in the Arts Council, the actual Council etc., wanted to keep it that way. They did not want the play to be produced, not now, not ever, and they were prepared to use all their power and influence to make sure that they won the argument.

Sam and Jimmy were equally determined to stage the play. The first hurdle they faced was Ritchie McKee, the chairman of the Group Theatre, who wanted to see the script. Jimmy objected saying that the reading committee had already seen and unanimously passed the play for production. He also said that they only had enough scripts for the cast and production company. Mr McKee was not going to be so easily fobbed off. In addition to being a successful businessman who was used to getting his own way, he was also very influential in the Arts scene, being Chairman of both the Group and the Arts Theatres, Chairman of CEMA, the forerunner to the present day Arts Council and the honorary position of Regional Governor of BBC NI. Outside of his involvement in the Arts he was a golfing partner of Lord Brookeborough, prime minister of Northern Ireland, and his brother was the Lord Mayor of Belfast. In other words not someone you wanted to annoy, especially if you worked in the theatre in Northern Ireland.

Safe in the knowledge that the play had been passed for production by the reading committee and that they had followed all the rules

James Ellis

laid down by the Group Theatre, Jimmy and Sam went ahead with rehearsals. On the first day Mr McKee's secretary appeared with a box-office girl in tow, saying that Mr McKee wanted to see the script. Jimmy gave the same answer of only enough copies for the cast, but after they left it was discovered that one of the scripts had disappeared. The next day the cast arrived to learn that rehearsals had been cancelled and that Jimmy and Maurice O'Callaghan [one of two actors' representatives on the board of the Group Theatre] were to attend an emergency meeting of the board. At the meeting the board voted by 6:2 to cancel the play. Their argument was that it would inflame sectarian tensions. Jimmy was later to say of himself and Maurice (both of whom were going to appear in the play),

> "I have often though over the years that Maurice, who came from a Catholic background ... and myself from a Protestant background ... virtually represented a metaphor for the play's non-sectarian stance; and here we were taking a mutual stand against a more insidious form of sectarianism, namely the withdrawal of the right to free speech."

It has gone down in history that the company resigned *en masse*, which is not true, but the resignation of Harold Goldblatt, and Jimmy[3] certainly made headlines. Ritchie McKee issued a statement to the press trying to give the board's version of events, but it read like an attempt at censorship and if he had thought that it would eventually die down he was very much mistaken.

Jimmy and the rest of the company were now even more determined to perform the play but where and when? The first thing to do was to form a new production company and so Ulster Bridge Productions was formed. The next problem was to find a venue.

---

3. Jimmy's resignation was delayed to allow him to fulfill the Group Theatre's commitment to their Bangor summer season, as he felt that it was not fair that it should be shelved, just because of a dispute in Belfast.

Famous Folk from Belfast

In this regard they were in luck. It was suggested that they should approach Frank Reynolds, the manager of the Empire Theatre in Victoria Square. It was an old Music Hall theatre, rather past its best but it had played host to famous names such as Marie Lloyd, Harry Lauder and Charlie Chaplin in it heyday. Most importantly the Findlater family in Dublin, who would not be so easily influenced to refuse the play, owned it. Jimmy's resolve to stage the play was strengthened by the support of Tyrone Guthrie.

It was a brave decision to proceed in the face of such opposition. By this time he was a married man and father of two, Amanda and Adam, as his opponents were quick to point out. Despite ever more pressure being brought to bear by those in a position to influence his career, Jimmy pressed on with the production and despite all the odds the play progressed through rehearsals and problems with the structure of the stage, which couldn't bear the weight of the set and had to be repaired. As the date of the first night approached there was more and more press interest. Generally it was swinging in favour of the production and against what was seen as censorship, but success was by no means guaranteed. While they had tried to keep costs to a minimum the stage design included scaffolding and called for many extras. It was here that Guthrie stepped in and told them that he should approach the Lord Carson Memorial Flute Band, who he had used the previous year in a production of *The Bonefire*. This was an inspired move of which Jimmy would later say *'When their voices were raised individually or collectively, it was the authentic sound of the docklands.'*

Finally, it was the 26th January 1960, opening night. There was a significant police presence, due to 'establishment' fears that the play would lead to riots, but the queue of shipyard workers and their wives, there to see 'their' play were well behaved. As the curtain fell at the end of the play the theatre erupted with applause. The play was a great success as it turned out that the public did not want to be told what they could or could not see. In his autobiography Jimmy recounted that in the first week of the production they received a phone call on behalf of the Governor of Northern Ireland, Lord Wakehurst asking if he could have two tickets. After the show, Lord and Lady Wakehurst came backstage to meet the cast and have a couple of drinks and he commented that he really couldn't see why there had been such a fuss about the play. Jimmy was later told that a few weeks later Lord Wakehurst happened to be at an official function when he spotted Ritchie McKee and called out *"Any riots yet McKee?"*

The public reaction was one of universal acclaim, and church leaders congratulated the play's plea for tolerance. The public continued to flock to the theatre and the run had to be extended. Well over forty thousand people had flocked to see the play in Belfast over a six-week period. Many of them had never seen a play before and in many ways the fact that they had had to put it on in an old Music Hall worked to their advantage. If it had gone ahead at the Group or the Grand Opera House, many of the shipyard workers would have felt that it wasn't for them. The plan had been to take it to Dublin after the Belfast run had ended but they ended up having to find and rehearse a new company and put it on at the same time. Then they were approached by the Laurence Olivier Production Company to stage the play in London[4] and Granada Television asked for the rights to film the play.

While Jimmy had undoubtedly won the battle, he had not won the war, and it soon became apparent that if he wanted to continue a career in acting he would have to leave Ireland. *'I had 'offended' – against the establishment, that is – and for this reason was 'persona non grata''*

---

4. The translation to the West End was not a success as the London audience found it hard to understand the thick accents and shipyard humour.

Famous Folk from Belfast

He moved to London and managed to get himself an agent. His first audition was at the BBC where he was delighted to see that one of the interviewers was a familiar face from BBC NI, Ronald Mason. The play was *The Randy Dandy* and he won the part. He was also given a part in the Granada Television production of *Over the Bridge,* along with an Irish actor called Donal Donnely. Donnely asked him if he would like to flat-share with a number of other Irish actors, all trying to get work in London. This was to change his life as Donal, unable to take the role himself, suggested Jimmy as a replacement in a new crime drama series at the BBC. The series was called *Crime Patrol* but was later changed to *Z Cars* and the character was called PC McGinty. Jimmy thought the name was too 'stage-Irish' and got it changed to PC Bert Lynch.

It is impossible for anyone born in the digital age, with hundreds of channels available on TV, computer, tablet or phone, to understand what it was like in the early 1960s when there were only two TV channels. TV ownership was beginning to increase so the viewing figures for popular dramas were huge. It literally emptied the streets as everyone from the Queen down tuned in twice a week. As Ivan Little reported[5] '*Z cars may have been broadcast in black and white but … it brought colour into millions of homes*'. It also made Jimmy a household name and enabled him to move his growing family over to join him in England. He was to remain in the series throughout its sixteen years, as Bert Lynch was promoted from PC to Inspector, never losing his accent.

Although he was now an established actor in England, he never forgot his home and would take every opportunity to return. He was also eager to help aspiring young actors and playwrights from his hometown. Of all his later work, perhaps the most famous (at least in Northern Ireland) was the *Billy* trilogy of plays by Graham

---

5. *Belfast Telegraph* 10 March 2014

James Ellis

Reid. He played the violent, troubled father Norman Martin opposite a young actor with Belfast roots, Kenneth Brannagh. When Jimmy died, Kenneth Brannagh paid tribute to his generosity as both a man and an actor,

> *"James Ellis was a great inspiration to me, and many other actors from the North of Ireland. I was blessed to begin my career working with him, and I will never forget his generosity to me. He was a highly intelligent, funny and kind man, and a tremendous actor."*

While his career continued to prosper, sadly his first marriage broke up in the late 1960s and he later married his second wife Robina in 1976. He was a very proud father to his daughter Amanda and sons Adam, Hugo and Toto. Adam's murder, at the age of 28, nearly broke him. Adam had been fishing on a towpath in London when a stranger demanded money. In the subsequent struggle he was stabbed and bled to death before help could arrive. Jimmy had to identify his body. Then twenty or so years later his second son Hugo, who had struggled with mental health issues, committed suicide.

We remember Jimmy today as an actor, and indeed he was still working at 81 starring as a care home resident in *Eternal Law*. However acting was only one string to his bow. He had not fluked his scholarship to Methody all those years ago, and he was a talented writer, poet and translated Greek and French poems into English. He was also an enthusiastic cricketer and often turned out for the Lord Taverners. As he never tired of telling people:

> *"...even if I say so myself, I was quite a nifty fielder close to the wicket. Somewhere in the vaults of the Lord Taverners headquarters there is an old scorebook that includes a dismissal that reads: DCS Compton c JM Parks b. J Ellis"*

James Ellis always remembered where he came from. He was proud to be from Belfast and always called it 'home'. He was happiest

Famous Folk from Belfast

when meeting up with old friends and family[6] for a chat and a catch-up. He was an enthusiastic supporter of the Arts in Belfast and received an honorary doctorate for services to the performing arts from Queen's in 2008. He died on the 8 March 2014.

He ends his autobiographical account of the play that made his name, *Troubles Over The Bridge*, with one of his own poems. The final lines of which read:

> *The hills of Antrim etched upon my heart,*
> *For, truth to tell, I never really left.*

---

6. A friend told me that his aunt, Mary, was Jimmy's uncle Joe Millar's widow. He would come over to visit every couple of months to take her out for a meal and a catch-up.

WILLIAM AND MARGARET PIRRIE
1847-1924 & 1857-1935
Shipbuilding and Philanthropy

William Pirrie was Chairman of Harland and Wolff during its heyday when it built some of the greatest ships in the world including the Titanic. His wife Margaret was an equally high achiever and was the main driving force in the establishment of the Royal Victoria Hospital.

On 12 July 1921 the *London Gazette* announced:

> To be a Viscount: The Rt. Hon. Sir William James, Baron Pirrie K.P., LL.D., D.L For Valuable services to the Government in connection with ship-construction during the war. Charitable work in connection with the Royal Victoria and other hospitals.

None of their family or friends, not least William himself, was in any doubt that the second part of the citation referred to William's wife, Margaret. They were very much a partnership and were only separated by his death in 1924, so I do not intend to separate them in this chapter.

William was born in 1847 in Quebec, while his parents [James Alexander and Eliza Swan née Montgomery] were staying in Canada, returning to the family home in Conlig, Co. Down at the age of 2. He was later educated at R.B.A.I [Inst] where he

Famous Folk from Belfast

was taught by the head of the English school[1], his uncle, Mr John Carlisle. Mr Carlisle had several children but we are only concerned with two of them. One son, Alexander Carlisle, who became the principal maritime architect at Harland and Wolffe, and a daughter, Margaret Montgomery Carlisle, who in 1879 married her first cousin[2] and became Mrs William Pirrie.

William's paternal grandfather, Captain William Pirrie, had been in charge of a Mediterranean trading ship during the Napoleonic wars and as Chairman on the Harbour Board was on the committee responsible for the drainage of Belfast Harbour[3] in the early decades of the century, so it did not come as a great surprise when William decided to take up what was referred to as a 'gentleman's apprenticeship' at the local Harland and Wolff shipyard in 1862, just a year after Edward Harland and Gustav Wolff had formed their famous partnership. Despite the description, this was no gilded shortcut to the top. William received a thorough grounding in all aspects of life at the yard, not only in Belfast but also in Greenock on the Clyde, Glasgow, where he learnt marine engineering. His realisation of the importance of this grounding was evident almost 30 years later when his nephew Thomas Andrews became an apprenticeship at the same yard and William insisted *'that no favour whatever was to be shown the boy on the score of relationship. By his own efforts and abilities he must make his way'*[4]

Once his apprenticeship had finished, William steadily worked his way up through the rapidly growing business until in 1874, having

---

1. Until 1898, when Robert Dods was appointed as Principal, Inst did not have a Headmaster. Rather there was a Board of Masters, made up of the Heads of the various 'Schools'.
2. Their mothers were sisters.
3. Upon the completion of the Victoria Channel in 1849 he celebrated by pouring either a bottle of whiskey or a bottle of champagne [depending on which source you chose] into the water.
4. Bullock 1865-1935, Shan F.. *Thomas Andrews, Shipbuilder*

been appointed Head Draughtsman, along with General Manager Walter Wilson he was made a partner by Edward Harland and Gustav Wolff.

While there is 'an embarrassment of riches' available about the life and achievements of William available in print and online, finding out information about Margaret's life is rather more difficult. And this is despite the fact that William himself often publicly credited her with a leading role in his career. In fact, despite dominating public and philanthropic life in Belfast in the decades following her marriage, including being the driving force behind the funding of the Royal Victoria Hospital, a seat on the Senate of the Queen's University of Belfast, being a leading advocate for women's suffrage and, following the death of William, being the President of Harland and Wolff to name but a few achievements, she merits a scant four lines in the Dictionary of Ulster Biography and you will search in vain for her name in many a reputable history of Belfast.

A large part of William's success as a businessman was his personality and his ability to charm. As Jonathan Bardon notes:

> 'Ebullient and daring, he set out with dazzling skill and energy to win new orders for the firm at a time of acute depression in the industry.'

However his business methods could be somewhat unorthodox such as offering credit to prospective clients on the understanding that the yard would be used for all repairs and upgrades, thus ensuring repeat business. Together William and Margaret used their ever-expanding social circle to help oil the wheels in the growth of Harland and Wolff's business[5] and entertained prospective cli-

---

5. It was at one such dinner party at their London residence, Downshire House, that plans for Titanic and Olympia were first discussed with Joseph Bruce Ismay of the White Star Line.

ents at intimate dinners in their homes. An oft-repeated story of William's sales prowess was that of a Liverpool ship-owner who was reputed to have confided in a friend that: *"Pirrie has just persuaded me to order a ship and I don't know what the deuce I'll do with it."*

William and Margaret were unable to have any children and the author of her short biography in the Ulster-Scots Community Network's *Herstory 2* opines that it was this that meant that:

> '*she took an unusually and exceptionally close interest in her husband's career. She accompanied him on business trips, visited the shipyard and familiarized herself with the yard's operation and company's finance.*'

Margaret also devoted herself with causes close to her heart outside her marriage, including women's suffrage, women's education and the provision of health care for her home city. She was a close personal friend of both Isabella Tod and Margaret Byers and actively supported them in their various campaigns, sitting on committees and providing generous donations to their funds.

However, of all her causes the one for which she should be remembered most is the Royal Victoria Hospital. Belfast had a variety of hospitals but most operated out of antiquated buildings and were not 'fit for purpose'. The idea for a new modern hospital was first proposed during William's year as Lord Mayor, 1896, and he and Margaret started off the fund-raising with donations of £5,000 and £2,000[6] respectively. Margaret threw herself into fund-raising and not only raised over £10,000 [£1.2 million] for Ward 5 but also raised £100,000 [over £12 million] in little over a year, by persuading people to fund individual beds. When the resulting hospital was opened[7] in 1903 by Edward VII and the king paid tribute to

---

6. £600,000 and £243,000 in today's money.
7. Debt free thanks to a further donation of £11,000 from the Pirries,

Viscount and Lady Pirrie

William for all his 'great work' someone on the platform party was heard to quip *"Yes, his wife collected the money."*

Margaret's involvement with the hospital continued until her death. She had already persuaded the Earl of Shaftesbury to donate the land upon which it was build, but she continued to campaign for donations and raised another £100,000 to endow the hospital, thus helping it to meet its running costs and allow for expansion. Her involvement was not just restricted to fund-raising and she chaired both the Ladies Committee[8] and the Nursing Committee and was President of the Hospital until her death.

All of Margaret's philanthropy was possible thanks to William's success as a businessman. Thanks largely to his success as a salesman by 1900 Harland and Wolff extended over 80 acres and employed over ten thousand men. He was in control of one of the leading shipyards in the world, and much of the heavy industry in Belfast was linked to its success. It was not unusual then that William should be attracted to public office and he was proud to serve as Lord Mayor of Belfast in 1896/7. In addition he was appointed as a Privy Counsellor (Ireland) in 1897 and High Sherriff of Co. Antrim in 1898, made Baron Pirrie in 1906, a Knight of the Order of St Patrick in 1908 and Pro-chancellor of QUB from 1908-14 as well as serving on the Committee of Irish Finance. Margaret was the first woman to be made an honorary burgess of Belfast in 1904.

The closing decades of the nineteenth century and first decades of the twentieth were dominated in Ireland by the three proposed Home Rule bills, introduced by successive Liberal governments in London. Initially, like many prominent Ulster industrialists, William and Margaret were opposed to Home Rule from an economic stand-point. They feared that the industrial north of Ireland

---
8. A fellow committee member was Margaret Byers of Victoria College.

would not prosper if ruled from Dublin and worried that it would lead to a complete breakup of the political and economic union with not only the United Kingdom but also the rest of the British Empire [and her markets]. They had been supporters of the Liberal party and, like Isabella Tod and Margaret Byers, were appalled by what they saw as a betrayal of their loyalty. In this they were not driven by sectarianism, but rather hard economic pragmatism.

Gradually, however, William's views began to change and he found himself agreeing to the Ulster Liberal Association's argument that the devolving of certain political powers away from centralized government might be beneficial and that:

> 'We are true Unionists in the best sense of the word. A sullen discontented Ireland is a source of weakness; a contented, pacified and prosperous Ireland will give us a new strength and solidarity. Only a large and generous measure of Home Rule can achieve that happy result'.

This perceived change in political allegiance lost them many friends both at home and in London. In his diary of 17 January 1913[9], Cecil Craig noted an embarrassing incident with the great political hostess, Theresa, Lady Londonderry:

> 'One day of the terrace of the House of Commons, Lady Pirrie, whose husband had ratted to the other side, rushed up to her and after greeting her said 'what very changeable weather we are having.' Lady [Londonderry] sniffed loudly and replied "I dislike change of any sort." And turned her back on her.'

Margaret had already endured worse barbs and even physical assault as occurred on 12 February 1912 when she and William were attacked by a mob as they tried to board a ferry at Larne. Conor Morrissey notes that despite being:

---

9. PRONI D-1415/B/38

Viscount and Lady Pirrie

'Protected by just six policemen, the crowd rushed the couple, whom they pelted with rotten eggs, herrings, and bags of flour.'

As they sheltered from the mob William and Margaret could not foresee that the following months were to bring greater disaster to the family. A few years earlier at a dinner in their Belgravia home, Downshire House, William had discussed with the directors of the White Star Line [with whom Harland and Wolff had long had a successful association dating back to the 1860s] the possibility of building a new class of trans-Atlantic passenger liner. This led to the yard building probably the most famous [or infamous] ship in the world – *RMS Titanic*. She was launched with great fanfare in Belfast and set off from Southampton on her maiden voyage on 10 April 1912. William and Margaret were supposed to be on board but William was ill and so they did not accompany their nephew, Thomas Andrews, and the approximately 2,200 other passengers and crew to cross the Atlantic. The loss of the ship was a personal tragedy as William and Margaret were very close to their nephew who had followed his uncle into Harland and Wolff. With no children of their own, he would have seemed to be his uncle's natural heir to take over leadership at the yard they both loved so much. While the subsequent public enquiries on both sides of the Atlantic exonerated the company it is impossible to believe that the terrible loss of life did not continue to haunt them both.

The First World War saw an upswing in production at Harland and Wolff and also more responsibility for William as he was co-opted on to the War Office Supply Board. In March 1918 he was appointed controller-general of merchant shipbuilding and raised production by almost 50 per cent by the end of the war. Bardon records that:

'During 1918 alone, Harland and Wolff launched 201,070 tons of merchant shipping, 120,000 tons more than the firm's nearest United Kingdom rival.'

Famous Folk from Belfast

According to Moss and Hume[10] the firm broke all records in completing standard ships and cite the example of how a ship could be launched from Queen's Island on the morning of one day and by 9pm the following day be ready for sea. In November 1918, in the week of the armistice, William set out his hopes for the future telling the shipyard workers that:

> *The war is over in the Fields, but not in the Shipyards. Germany is beaten but she cannot give us back all the shipping she has destroyed ... there must be no slacking of effort in shipbuilding as ships are as vitally necessary today as at any period in the history of this country.*

And he was to deliver on his aspirations as, despite an unsettled period in both labour relations and national politics, he expanded the workforce to almost 30,000 and opened a new 'east' yard with more capacity than the north and south yards combined. However despite all the optimism events would soon take a turn for the worse.

While on a business trip to explore possible Latin-American tourist routes that William contracted bronchial pneumonia and passed away on 7 June 1924. I have been unable to discover whether or not Margaret was with him. His body was brought home onboard the White Star ship *RMS Olympic*, built by Harland and Wolff, and his loss was greatly regretted, not least by his constant companion Margaret. Hugh Pollock, the finance minister of the new Northern Ireland government paid tribute to him saying that he was

> *"a veritable Napoleon of industry in the greatness and splendor of the schemes which had .. taken form in his mind".*

However, William's apparent success was qualified by the way in which it was being financed. After William's death his successor, Sir Owen Cosby Philipps, Baron Kylsant [who at William's instigation

---

10. Michael Moss and John R Hume *Shipbuilders to the World: 125 years of Harland and Wolff*, Belfast 1861-1986 Belfast, 1986

Viscount and Lady Pirrie

had become the majority shareholder in the business] was horrified to discover that William had been, shall we say, somewhat creative when compiling the company's accounts. With an overdraft of almost £3 million [almost £181 million today] and all the ships in its apparently healthy order book contracted at prices less than they would cost to build, Harland and Wolff was essentially bankrupt. Margaret, who was Honorary President of the company, was very protective of her late husband's legacy and his memory which led to her clashing with Kylsant.

Facing financial ruin, Kylsant attempted to hide the truth from the creditors and the world at large but the methods he employed to try to rectify the situation were somewhat less successful than Pirrie's and would see him jailed for fraud in 1931.

Margaret continued to involve herself in all her committees. Two years before William's death, she had become the first woman Justice of the Peace in Belfast and two years after his death she became an honorary member of the Belfast Chamber of Commerce, and of course her active involvement with the Royal Victoria Hospital continued to take up most of her time. She died at her home in London on 19 June 1935.

While the Harland and Wolff business did not bear his name, for many years William Pirrie *was* Harland and Wolff. Without his drive and vision and Margaret's whole-hearted support and advice, it would not have dominated world shipbuilding in the late nineteenth and early twentieth centuries. William always acknowledged Margaret's vital role in his success and her influence was noted by others. I will leave the final word on the dynamic Pirries to the Marquess of Dufferin and Ava who, talking about Margaret, said:

> "she is the most charming and most popular lady mayoress who has ever sceptered a city or disciplined a husband."

WINNIFRED CARNEY
1887-1943

Trade Unionist, Suffragette, Republican

A fervent socialist, Winnifred was both heavily involved in both the Trades Union and the Republican movements. She was James Connolly' secretary in the run up to and during the Easter rising and, armed with both a typewriter and a Webley revolver, was at Connolly's side as he entered the GPO on O'Connell Street.

Winifred Carney was born in the family home on Fisher's Hill [Victoria Road], Bangor on the 4 December 1887, the youngest of seven children born to Alfred Carney and his wife Sarah Cassidy. Both her parents had been brought up in Belfast, but theirs was a mixed marriage and her father, at least on the marriage certificate, had converted to Catholicism so perhaps they thought that it would be easier to bring their young family up in the less sectarian Co. Down seaside resort. Whatever the reason, the family did not stay long in Bangor and by the time of the 1891 census the family were living in Fulham, London where Alfred is listed as being a commission agent. The marriage broke down at some stage over the next decade and by 1901 Sarah is listed as being the head of the household and living with her children in Perth Street, Belfast. Winnie (as she was always called) was still at school at the Christian Brothers School on Donegall Street. The family

Winnifred Carney

made their final move a few years later to Carlisle Circus, where Sarah opened a small sweet shop.

For many young girls from single parent families at the turn of the twentieth century the more usual choice of employment was factory work in one of the hundreds of factories in the heart of Belfast. Winnie, however, was determined to resist this course and enrolled in the Hughes Commercial Academy, where she became one of the first women to qualify as a shorthand typist. This qualification opened up a whole world of possibilities to her and also the chance of earning her own living. One of her first jobs was as a clerk in a solicitor's office in Dungannon, although by 1911 she was back in Belfast.

While still in her early twenties she had become very interested in both nationalist politics and social reform. Her mother Sarah was a supporter of John Redmond's Irish Parliamentary Party and the whole family had been actively involved in the Gaelic Revival that sought to establish a national cultural identity. Winnie also became involved in the woman's suffrage movement, joining the Irish Women's Suffrage Society and trade union movements. She became friends with Marie Johnston, whose husband Thomas became a leader of the Irish Labour Party, and Delia Larkin, sister of labour leader James Larkin[1]. It was her friendship with both of these women that was to change her life.

---

1. James Larkin was born in Liverpool to Irish Parents. A member of the Independent Labour Party, despite it costing him his job as a foreman in the Liverpool Docks, he helped to organize a National Union of Dock Workers' led strike. Arriving in Belfast in 1907 he successfully unionised the Belfast dock workers and called a strike for better working conditions and wages in June 1907. It was called off in November the same year without achieving his aims. He moved on to Dublin. He was not universally endorsed by local political and social radicals with no less a person than Arthur Griffith, founder of Sinn Fein, described him as an *'Englishman importing foreign political disruption into this country and putting native industry at risk.'*

Famous Folk from Belfast

Together with Delia Larkin she was a founding member of the Irish Textile Workers' Union, which was the female counterpart to the Irish Transport and General Workers Union, led by James Connolly. Working conditions for men and women in the factories of Belfast were pretty grim. Unlike many industrial cities elsewhere, there was a great demand for women workers in the linen and textile mills but this demand did not lead to improved wages or working conditions. Management in many of the mills operated a 'fine' system where any infraction of a long list of, in most cases, petty rules could result in quite substantial reductions or fines in the weekly wage packet. Fines could and were imposed for talking, laughing and singing, as well as being late for work. There was no such thing as a 'living wage' and women were paid considerably less than their male counterparts.[2]

It was through her friendship with Marie Johnston that Winnie was introduced to James Connolly. Marie had been working as Connolly's secretary but in 1912 ill health had meant that she was going to have to give up work. She suggested that her friend Winnie would make a good replacement. Having met Connolly and being inspired by his commitment to socialist principles and despite, ironically, having to take quite a substantial pay-cut[3], Winnie agreed. She began by helping the workers to pay their dues under the National Insurance Act of 1911. This was a rudimentary step towards the Welfare State and National Health Service, which enabled workers to obtain health and unemployment benefits through contributions shared between the employer, employee and government. However, to receive it you had to be registered and Winnie was active in promoting workers to do so.

---

2. Despite numerous acts of parliament throughout the twentieth century, sadly, this still happens, even in the BBC.

3. Winnie told Connolly's daughter Nora that she had given up 10 shillings a week to work for just 5 shillings for Connolly.

Winnifred Carney

Together with Connolly's daughters Ina and Nell, she helped to draught the 1913 Manifesto to Irish Textile workers, which was a call to arms to the *Sweated Women of all Classes of Labour*, especially the spinners, pointing out that:

> '*a qualified spinner in Belfast receives a wage less than some of our pious mill owners would spend weekly upon a dog.*'

They called for what they called the Sweated Industries Act[4] to be extended to textile workers and urged women to organize and unionise.

Working closely with Connolly, in fact closer than anyone else, it was not a surprise that she would have become more and more convinced by his political aspirations for Irish independence and republicanism. In 1912 she joined Na Fianna Éireann, a nationalist youth movement and later was one of the first members of Nora and Ina Connolly's Young Republican Movement.

In early September 1913, Connolly was arrested for his involvement with the increasingly violent industrial turmoil in Dublin, when there was an employers' lock out of all union members. He was refused bail and immediately went on hunger strike. Unlike suffragette hunger strikers, no attempts were made to force feed him, but he was released later in the month and returned to Belfast. Winnie organized a reception committee made up of mill workers, who accompanied him from the Great Northern Railway station to the union headquarters in York Street.

The industrial unrest in Dublin, which was accompanied by real deprivation for the families of the striking workers, led to Larkin, Connolly and Countess Constance Markievicz [an Anglo-Irish aristrocrat] amongst others forming the Irish Citizen Army in

---

4. The Trade Boards Act of 1909, proposed by Winston Churchill, created boards to set a minimum 'living' wage for certain workers. It was expanded in 1912 to include miners but not textile workers.

Famous Folk from Belfast

November 1913. The constitution of the ICA stated that members [of both sexes] should fight for an Irish Republic and for the emancipation of labour. A few weeks later, in an attempt to steer away from extremism, the Irish Volunteer Force was formed on 25 November 1913 to safeguard Home Rule. It was inspired by and organized along the same lines as the already well established Ulster Volunteer Force. The fact that some of the leading members were the same employers who had instigated the Dublin lock-out, inevitably lead to conflict with the ICA.

By the start of 1914 there were four paramilitary 'armies' openly parading and training in Ireland, two on each side of the Home Rule debate. In March 1914 there was a very good reason to think that the UVF were going to attack Carrickfergus Castle, to try to seize its munitions. The government, determined to prevent this ordered the regiments stationed at the Curragh Barracks north to defend the castle only for the officers of the regiments to resign their commissions and most of the soldiers to refuse to obey orders. There was a very real threat of civil war and it was only a matter of time before someone would provide them with guns, and so enters Fred Crawford[5]. With the tacit agreement of amongst others Edward Carson, Crawford had travelled to Hamburg to try to buy around 40,000 rifles and over three and a half million rounds of ammunition. He then acquired a boat *Fanny*, which was renamed *Doreen* and attempted to smuggle the guns into an Ulster port. Frustrated with the efforts of the Royal Navy to prevent his mission he arranged for the guns to be transferred on to a coal boat, *Clyde Valley*, which was renamed *Mountjoy*, and during the hours of darkness between the 24 and 25 of April the guns were successfully off loaded at Larne, Bangor and Donaghadee and distributed throughout the northern counties. In an attempt to shut the gate

---

5. To read the full story I would highly recommend Keith Haines's excellent book *Fred Crawford: Carson's Gunrunner* published by Cottage Publications.

after the horse had bolted the government banned all importation of guns into Ireland, a move that Connolly saw as an attempt to prevent the ICA and IVF from following suit. He also saw it as a betrayal of the government's own commitment to Home Rule and *'that they connive at these illegalities that they might have an excuse for their betrayal.*[6]*'*

While Connolly was spending increasing amounts of time in Dublin, Winnie took over effective control of running the ITGWU, doing all the clerical work for the union in addition to her previous job in the insurance section. While in theory her weekly wage was raised to £1, in reality the union finances were so precarious that despite juggling money between accounts she often sacrificed her own wages to help others. She had also joined the Women's Social and Political Union, where she would have met Dr Elizabeth Bell, although she did not take an active part in their increasing militancy.[7] She joined the Belfast branch of Cumann na mBan , the League of Women, and helped to organize fundraising dances and concerts. Cumann na mBan also ran first aid classes and rifle and revolver training. Prior to the Larne gunrunning incident Winnie had been ambivalent about the use of arms but by the time the IVF landed guns at Howth she had changed her mind. While she had not been present her friends, Nora and Ina, were there and brought two rifles back with them to Belfast.

Belfast on 28 July 1914 appeared to be hovering on the brink of a civil war. Then an Austrian Archduke and his wife were killed in Sarajevo. Unionist politicians had managed to secure an amendment to the Home Rule bill which would have temporarily ex-

---

6. 'The Liberals and Ulster', from *Forward* 30 May 1914
7. Many suffragettes felt betrayed by the Unionist leadership. Carson had promised full suffrage for women but had backtracked upon the pledge. As a result many of the WSPU arson attacks were directed at Unionist owned buildings as well as golf clubs and other sporting clubs that excluded women.

cluded Ulster from the act but at the outbreak of war both the amendment and the bill were shelved. While the members of the UVF and more than 180,000 members of the IVF, renamed the National Volunteers, flocked to enlist, each convinced that doing so would lend weight to their arguments after the armistice, Connolly was convinced that this was the time to fight, not for Home Rule, but for independence.

Around 13,000 members of the IVF had opposed their leaders' support for the war and they now coalesced around a general council of fifty members including Patrick Pearse, Bulmer Hobson, and Joseph Plunkett. As the war progressed, Connolly became increasingly frustrated by the lack of progress in taking advantage of the situation. Unaware of the efforts of general council to obtain support for an uprising from Germany and among the Irish American community, Connolly at the start of 1916 told the readers of *The Workers' Republic* that they were: *rebels in heart, and ...that opportunities are for those who seize them, and that the coming year may be as bright as we choose to make it.* The IVF leadership were alarmed that he might organize his own uprising, and so at the end of January made him aware of their own plans. Once he knew he shared the information with Winnie. He had been appointed military commander of republican forces in Dublin.

Winnie was still in Belfast on Friday, 14 April 1916 when she received a telegram from Connolly asking her to come to Dublin on the afternoon train. On Sunday, 16 April she was by his side as he hoisted a flag with the words 'Irish Republic' over Liberty Hall[8]. From this point onwards to the actual rising on 24 April, Winnie was rarely away from Connolly's side, notebook in hand, taking down his orders and typing them out, including typing the Proclamation of the Irish Republic.

---

8. A former hotel 'Liberty Hall' had been the headquarters of the ITGWU, IWWU and The *Irish Worker* as well as the ICA

Winnifred Carney

The Easter Rising very nearly didn't happen. Roger Casement had been arrested, the German merchant ship *Aud* which was carrying 20,000 rifles had been intercepted and the administration in Dublin Castle were well informed about the plans. However, their plans to arrest the leaders at Liberty Hall were thwarted as the telegram from London giving permission to proceed was delayed because of Easter Sunday and only arrived after the rising had started on the Monday. Due to conflicting instructions coming from the leadership of the Rising, fewer men and women were mobilized on Easter Monday, but Winnie, armed with both a typewriter and a Webley revolver was by Connolly's side as he entered the GPO on O'Connell Street. "*We halt outside the GPO. Connolly giving the order, and we quickly march inside.*" She later remembered how, after the Tricolour was hoisted over the GPO, Connolly took her outside to see it and to listen as Patrick Pearse read the Proclamation outside the building.

As the administration finally organized an armed response to the rising, Winnie remained by Connolly's side throughout the next few days. To keep up morale Connolly encouraged those inside the GPO to sing songs, much to Michael Collins' disgust. Connolly was hit by a bullet, that shattered his ankle and for the first time Winnie refused to do as he told her and remained by his side until they were both evacuated from the burning building, among the last group to leave for Moore Street. It was at Moore Street that Patrick Pearse surrendered and Connolly and Winnie were arrested.

Following her arrest Winnie was held overnight at the Rotunda before being moved, first to the Richmond Barrack and then to Kilmainham jail. It was while she was being held here that:

> *In the early morning of May 3 I am awakened by the sound of firing ... My heart sinks for I know the first of the executions has begun ...*

Famous Folk from Belfast

But for many mornings to come we shall awake to that close noise of rifle firing and the crisp voice of the officer in command.

The last of the executions was that of James Connolly who was tied to a chair as he could not stand on his shattered ankle.

On 20 June, Winnie along with Nell Ryan, Helena Molony, Marie Perolz, and Brigid Foley were sent to Lewes Prison in Sussex. Foley and Perolz were released on appeal by Nell, Helena and Winnie were transferred to the political prisoners' wing of Aylesbury Prison, the same prison as Countess Markievicz although she was being held as an ordinary criminal. Winnie tried to give up her political prisoner status to join the Countess but was refused.

She was released on Christmas Eve and returned to Liberty Hall on Christmas Day to be reunited with Nora and shortly afterwards she returned to her mother's house in Carlisle Circus and took up her work for the ITGWU, the Workers' Educational Association and Cumann na mBan, representing Belfast at their convention. She and her mother got so used to RIC raids on their home, in search of seditious material, that she took to sleeping in her clothes.

While her hopes for an independent Ireland were put on hold for the moment, she was delighted when, following the end of the war, women over thirty were awarded the vote and she worked tirelessly to make sure as many of the mill workers were registered as possible. Winnie was one of only two women candidates selected by Sinn Fein for the forthcoming election in Ireland. The other woman was Countess Constance Markievicz, who successfully stood in Dublin, thus becoming the first woman elected to Parliament, although she refused to take her seat.

Winnie stood in the staunchly Unionist Victoria Division. Although her nomination papers were signed by docker John Quinn and a barber called Andrew Leonard, and despite all her hard work for the men of the ITGWU and presence in the GPO

Winnifred Carney

during the rising, she discovered that their commitment to equality did not include canvassing for women candidates, and so her election campaign was notable for the number of women who attended her public meetings, including the secretary of Cumann na mBann, Miss Cashel, Countess Plunkett, and her friend the poet Alice Milligan. She wrote an angry letter to Joe McGrath of Sinn Fein complaining that she had not been provided money for committee rooms, the deposit for the election or any canvassers and that as a consequence she was amazed to have received 395 votes.

Following her failed attempt at election, Winnie resumed her work for the union and also became secretary of the Irish Republican Prisoners' Dependents' Fund, and while she maintained her links with the ICA and received visits from Countest Markievicz, amongst others, she felt that the Socialist Party of Ireland better reflected her own political aspirations rather than Sinn Fein. Her involvement in republican politics meant that she was of interest to the authorities and her house was often raided by the RIC. She was horrified by what she viewed as Michael Collins's betrayal when he signed the Anglo-Irish Treaty in December 1921. This compromise was not what she and Connolly had fought for, however she did act as a courier for messages between Michael Collins and Sir James Craig, the Prime Minister of the newly created Northern Ireland.[9] And gradually came to accept his argument that while the Treaty did not give them all they desired, it did give them the freedom to achieve it.

As Ireland raced towards a civil war, with republicans against unionists, pro-Treaty against anti-Treaty, once again Winnie was arrested, for actions against the state. She was moved to Armagh's Womens' Prison while she awaited procecusion for possession of

---

9. The resulting Craig-Collins pact, signed on 30 March 1922, lasted no more than 24 hours before it came under attack from both sides. Winnie was on the Committee that was formed to enact it.

Famous Folk from Belfast

IRA documents, under the Reg. 24.A. of Civil Authorities (Special Powers) Act but her health began to break down and when she appeared before the Magistrates on 9 August in Belfast she was so weak that she had to hold on to the dock to stop herself from collapse. She was fined 40 shillings and released.

In January 1924, Winnie, on the advice of a friend, joined the Court Ward branch of the Labour Party in North Belfast. She was delighted to see some old friends, but many of the members were younger than herself, including a young man with dark good looks. His name was George McBride. He was around 10 years younger than Winnie, he was a Protestant, a member of the UVF, an Orangeman, had fought in the Battle of the Somme and was as committed an Unionist as she was a Republican. They were both involved in helping to organize a demonstration against the Board of Poor Law Guardians to be held in Belfast the next month, and after the demonstration George asked if he could walk her home.

Over the next couple of years their friendship grew, much to the bemusement of both sets of friends, and largely hidden from their respective families. Neither could visit the other's home and while they both came to respect the others principles they never wavered from their own commitments. Where they did unite was in their commitment to the socialist cause, and they were both actively involved in Labour Party work, especially during the Workers' Strike of 1926. In September 1927, outside the Great Northern Railway station where over a decade before she had organized mill workers to greet Connolly, George asked Winnie to marry him and she said 'Yes'.

They were married in a civil ceremony on 26 September in Holyhead, Wales. No family attended as both were equally opposed to the match. They returned home to their new house in Whitewell Parade and while George returned to work in his

WINNIFRED CARNEY

new leather-goods' shop[10], Winnie became a housewife. Winnie's mother had been vehemently opposed to the marriage, but shortly after the event decided that if he was Winnie's choice then she would have to accept it, and months later she moved in with them. Winnie's sisters, both of whom were nuns, came round to the marriage, but her brothers remained implacable. So too did George's parents, although he always thought that if his mother hadn't died shortly after the marriage, she may have taken a similar line as Sarah, and his brother Jack did eventually reinstate cordial relations with the couple.

The last decade of Winnie's life was plagued by ill health as she gradually succumbed to tuberculosis, however both remained actively involved in workers rights, helping to organize the Outdoor Relief strike of 1932. She died in George's arms on the 21 November 1943. Ever practical, Winnie had organized her own funeral and a grief-stricken George was too overwhelmed to object when her brother Ernest arrived from Dublin and not only registered the grave in Millfield in his own name, but also removed many of Winnie's personal belongings from their home. The funeral, although small, did briefly unite both sides of the family and there were representatives from the Irish government and the many organisations for which she had worked. Ernest refused permission for a headstone to mark her grave as he did not want an Orangeman's name on it.

George continued to live in their old home until December 1978, when he moved into the UVF Hospital[11] in East Belfast. He was delighted when in December 1985, following a campaign by Belfast

---

10. For most of his adult life, George had worked at Mackies but felt that his workmates would not have accepted his marriage to a veteran of the GPO and so he had handed in his resignation before his marriage.

11. The UVF Hospital was based in Craigavon House, James Craig's home. During the First World War it was given up as a hospital for wounded soldiers. By the time George arrived it was a retirement home.

trade unionists, a headstone was erected in Milltown Cemetery for his beloved Winnie, which at least acknowledged that she was the *beloved wife of George McBride*. When George died on 21 April 1988 he was buried in the Clandeboye cemetery in Winnie's hometown of Bangor. Again it was at the behest of the trade unions to whom both Winnie and George had given so much commitment, that a headstone was erected in 2016 at a ceremony attended by both families.

Winnie was a woman of strong convictions. She never wavered in her loyalty to both the republican ideal that she had discussed with Connolly, or to her socialist principles. She was able to separate the sectarian from the political, and in that she was in the same tradition as MaryAnn McCracken. She lost friends and family because of her marriage, but she felt that it was their loss, not hers. She had the courage of her convictions, every bit as much on the day she said "I do" to George as in April 1916.

George had kept a scrapbook of all the obituaries written about her. In pride of place was one written by her friend Cathal O'Shannon in *The Torch*. I think it is apt to close this account of an extraordinary life with the closing paragraph:

> *Beneath her placid, almost timid exterior, there burned fires which could scorch when anybody provoked her ... Above all she was deep and loyal in her friendships and in her allegiances, political as well as personal ... And her friendship was intimate, understanding and selfless – she was a great and trusted custodian of confidences.*

Ruby Murray
1935-1996
Singer

The UK's top popular musician in the mid 1950s. In 1955 she had 10 singles in the top 20 at the same time, a feat only equalled (but not beaten) by Bill Hayley, Elvis and Michael Jackson

I am not exactly *au fait* with Cockney Rhyming Slang, but even I know that 'Going for a Ruby' means curry. So what is the connection between this phrase and Belfast?

The answer is simple. The Ruby concerned is Ruby Murray, one of the biggest selling singers of the 1950s and one of a select group of individual singers to have had 5 singles in the top 20 at the same time. To give an idea of how unusual this is, only Elvis and Madonna have equaled it. Obscured by the mists of time, it is hard to appreciate how big a star she was, but really all we need to know is that Frank Sinatra was one of her biggest fans.

Ruby was the youngest of four siblings and was born in the family home at 84 Moltke Street, just off the Donegall Road area of Belfast, on 29 March 1935. At the tender age of six weeks old she had to have an operation on severely swollen glands in her throat,

Famous Folk from Belfast

which left her with her distinctively husky voice. A family visit to a local music hall while only five years old is credited with inspiring Ruby to join a local children's choir, and within weeks she was performing solos. Everyone has heard about the dreaded 'Stage Mother' but in Ruby's case it was her father Dan who encouraged her on to the stage and he even promoted shows featuring his talented daughter. At the age of 12 she was spotted by Richard Afton, a television producer, and she made her debut on a BBC light entertainment show at Alexandra Palace. Then as now there were very strict rules about how many hours a child could work so her age debarred her from capitalizing on this early success. Even so, according to her first husband Bernie Burgess, after this appearance local promoters would advertise her as Ruby Murray – BBC Television Star.

Working within the strict rules, Ruby built up quite a reputation as a child star throughout the island of Ireland and even appeared in the Ulster Hall. By the time she was 14, she was able to leave school and (with her mother accompanying her as chaperone) take up a place in a series of local touring Variety shows. In 1954 one of these shows, *Yankee Doodle Blarney*, was playing at the Metropolitan Music Hall in London when, yet again, she came to the attention of Richard Afton. Afton was the producer of the highly successful light entertainment TV show *Quite Contrary* and was looking for a replacement for his resident female singer, Joan Regan. As Bernie Burgess recounts:

> 'She was an instant success. The impact of her very first television appearance was immense, she had captured the hearts of millions of television viewers'.

The Musical Director on *Quite Contrary*, Ray Martin, was also employed at Columbia Records and he was so impressed that he gave her a recording contract. To quote Bernie Burgess again: *A star was born, a bright shining star.*

Ruby Murray

To understand Ruby's meteoric rise to fame it is important to look at what life was like in the early 1950s. The country was beginning to emerge from the deprivation of the war years. Rationing was only ended on 4 July 1954 and the concept of 'teenagers' was just beginning to make its way across from America. While there had been a huge spike in the sales of television sets to watch the Queen's coronation on 2 June 1953, less than 40% of households owned or rented a set. For those that did, up until 22 September 1955 when ITV was launched, there was only one channel. In today's age of digital entertainment at the touch of a screen on your smart phone it is difficult to conceive of a world without music channels, but before the advent of the pirate radio ships such as *Caroline* in the 1960s and the BBC's Radio 1, the only radio station that catered to the 'youth' market was *Radio Luxembourg* with Pete Murray introducing the *The Top Twenty* at 11 pm every Sunday. So programmes such as *Quite Contrary* were the only opportunity for young people to see contemporary musicians from the comfort of their own homes. Ruby's appearance on the programme more or less guaranteed her a ready market for any record releases.

Ruby's first hit single was *Heartbeat*, which was released at the end of 1954. This was followed by what was to become her most famous, and only No. 1, song *Softly, Softly*. She dominated the Top Twenty in the early months of 1955 as Columbia released several of her singles at the same time. Thus is was that in March 1955 she became the first singer to have five different singles in the Top Twenty at the same time. This is an amazing feat and is one that has only been equalled, but never surpassed in the subsequent decades. In fact the official Ruby Murray website[1], states that only Bill

---

1. www.rubymurray.org

Famous Folk from Belfast

Hayley, Elvis and Michael Jackson have equalled the achievement and that she remains the only female artist to hold the record.[2]

The five records were: *Heartbeat; Softly, Softly; Happy Days and Lonely Nights; Let me go, Lover;* and *If Anyone Finds This, I Love You,* all of which spent time in the Top Ten. She had two further hits in 1955 *Evermore* and *I'll come when you call.* In fact for the whole of the year she had at least one record in the charts each week. Promoted by Belfast born Phil Solomon[3] her career rocketed. Such was her popularity that she was voted Britain's favourite female vocalist by the New Musical Express readership, beating second placed Alma Cogan by over a thousand votes. She also appeared with Norman Wisdom in the *Painting the Town* revue at the London Palladium and appeared in the Royal Variety Performance.

Her success continued the following year with a vocal appearance, singing *You are my first love,* in the film *It's Great to be Young* and made her acting debut as a chambermaid in *A Touch of the Sun* with the late, great Frankie Howard. She also made a successful concert tour of the United States. However, tastes were beginning to change in music as in fashion. Looking at photographs of Ruby from her glory years, dressed in formal cocktail dresses, her hair neatly 'permed' she looks much older than her actual age of 20. A new, exciting, young style of music was flowing over from America – rock and roll – and Ruby was unable to recreate her success of 1955/6, although she remained very popular.

---

2. The website states that: *'It has been claimed erroneously in some publications that Madonna and/or The Beatles and/or Elvis Presley broke Ruby's World Record but this is incorrect. Checking with The Guinness Book of Records it was indisputably stated that although these artists had many hit records they never beat the World Record of having 5 recordings in the Top Twenty all in the same one week period.'* www.rubymurray.org

3. Born in Belfast in 1926, Solomon was a very successful entertainment promoter whose 'stable' included Cliff Richards, The Bachelors, Frank Carson and Phil Coulter. He owned several record companies and had a controlling interest in Radio Caroline, that he used to promote the careers of his own clients.

Ruby Murray

Also, other aspects of life were beginning to assume more importance. In 1957, while appearing in a summer season in Blackpool she met a young man called Bernard Burgess and, after a whirlwind romance, they were married. A son, Tim, and daughter, Julie, soon followed and Ruby tried to juggle motherhood, marriage and performances in a busy life.

As is all too common when meteoric success comes early in life something had to give. For every Lulu, or Cilla, there is a Lena Zavaroni or Ruby Murray. She had always been plagued with dreadful nerves before every performance and in an age when the dangers were not recognised, she began to mix valium with alcohol, to help her step on to the stage. Despite continuing successful tours and stage and television appearances, she began a descent into alcohol dependence, which she was to battle for the rest of her life. She joined Alcoholics Anonymous and had two nervous breakdowns, which resulted in time in psychiatric hospitals. Her marriage was unable to survive and when she and Bernie divorced in 1977 he was awarded custody of their two children after allegations of physical violence, levelled against Ruby.

At the time of her divorce she was already in a relationship with a long time friend, the theatrical manager Ray Lamont, and they eventually married in the early 1990s. Addiction is a terrible disease and despite the efforts of her loving family and devoted friends, in and outside show business, Ruby continued to fight her demons. She was arrested in 1982 for being drunk and disorderly and the damage that had been inflicted upon her liver would eventually catch up with her. She died on 17 December 1996 from Liver cancer.

In his obituary to her in the *Independent*, Tom Vallance records the heartbreak of Ruby's later life:

> '*Still fondly remembered, she received a standing ovation in 1985 when she appeared in the concert 'Forty Years of Peace' in the presence*

Famous Folk from Belfast

of Princess Anne, but her final London appearance, at Brick Lane Music Hall in March 1993, revealed a frail, halting performer.'

Despite having had her greatest success over half a century ago, Ruby continues to be remembered by the people of her own home town. In this century she has been the subject of two different plays by Marie Jones and Michael Cameron and, of course, there is always Cockney Rhyming Slang.

Sir Crawford McCullagh
1868-1948
Businessman, Lord Mayor of Belfast

He helped to create the commercial centre of Belfast becoming the longest serving Lord Mayor in the United Kingdom. He guided Belfast through both World Wars and initiated a five minute silence in remembrance of the Fallen at the Battle of the Somme.

I must admit that until a few years ago I didn't really know that much about Sir Crawford McCullagh. I had seen the stained glass window in the City Hall, and I had heard relatives talking about the Classic cinema, but I hadn't really paid that much attention. All that changed when I received a phone call from a lady called Susan Cunningham, asking for my help to prepare a manuscript for publication. It turned out that the manuscript was a biography of her great-grandfather, Sir Crawford McCullagh. I am so glad that I agreed to help her as the story of his life was fascinating, a real self-made man who used his success to help the people of his adopted city.

Famous Folk from Belfast

Crawford McCullagh was the fifth of six children born to Robert McClave McCullough[1] and his wife Mary Jane Hawthorne. They were tenant farmers in the townland of Annaghdroghal, Co. Antrim, and rented 70 acres from a Colonel Waring. In 1870 they had to leave the property after a dispute with the Colonel about a proposed rent increase[2]. This was not uncommon in Ireland at this time. When the newly wed Robert and Mary Jane had moved into the farmhouse in 1858 it had been run down and the outhouses and farm buildings dilapidated. They had worked hard to improve both the buildings and the land, employing the latest advances in farming practices, but then found that because of their hard work, the land and houses were now deemed to be worth more rent money. Determined to fight his landlord, Robert went to court twice, and lost twice. Unwilling to pay the increased rent he left the property, but not before razing all the crops and leaving them to rot in the ditches.

Robert and Mary Jane moved to Aghalee, where they rented 90 acres from the Marquis of Hertford. The young Crawford spent a happy, if strictly religious childhood on the farm. He and his siblings all attended Upper Ballinderry National School, where they got a good grounding in the 3 Rs, and they were all expected to work on the farm and help around the house. His parents had decided that his older brother should go to university to study medicine, and so he was sent to Lurgan College, but it soon became clear that he was not cut out for medicine and instead he was

---

1. The reason for the change in spelling the surname has been lost in the mists of time. Both Robert and his brother, Rev. Joseph Crawford McCullough, used the old spelling, but most of Crawford's siblings used the new one. Unfortunately all Crawford's personal papers were burnt after his death by his daughter-in-law in a wanton act of historical vandalism and no-one in the family knows the answer.
2. This situation was changed in the 1881 Land Act which brought in the three Fs. Fair rent – fixed for 15 years. Free Sale – forced compensation from the landlord to the tenant for any improvements made or paid for by the tenant. Fixity of Tenure – if the rent was paid the tenant couldn't be evicted.

Sir Crawford McCullagh

apprenticed as a trainee accountant with William Boyd & Sons, Londonderry.

Crawford's parents had decided that he should follow his uncle, and namesake, Rev Joseph Crawford McCullough, into the Presbyterian ministry and so he was dispatched to live in Bangor, where his uncle was minister at First Bangor Presbyterian. Exposed to the reality of life in a manse, Crawford was beginning to think that he may not be cut out for the ministry and when his aunt took him on a shopping trip to Belfast the experience changed his life.

He returned to the family farm and informed his parents that the ministry was not for him and that he wanted to go to Belfast to work in a shop. His parents were not amused and told him that if he wasn't going to be a minister he could be a farmer. A few month's later his brother, Sam, sent him a letter enclosing an advert, cut from the *Belfast News Letter*:

> *Wanted: Well educated boy as apprentice to the drapery trade. Apply Messrs, Robinson, Ledlie and Ferguson Co. Ltd., Bank Buildings, Castle Place, Belfast.*

Despite his father's strenuous objections, Crawford bought himself a return ticket to Belfast and applied, in person, for the position. He was accepted and only returned home to pack his things. He was moving to Belfast. He was 14 years old.

The terms of the apprenticeship seem rather harsh to modern eyes. He was expected to work, full-time, six days a week for five years in return for his board and lodgings. No money. Many boys were supported financially by their families but Crawford knew that his father would not help, and anyway he was determined not to ask. The life of an apprentice was hard. He lived in a dormitory shared with over twenty other apprentices in a property on Great Victoria Street and they were expected at the Bank Buildings by 8am where they would be given breakfast before starting work.

Famous Folk from Belfast

The shop opened at 9am, by which time the entire shop had been cleaned and polished by the apprentices. Time was spent learning their trade in each of the departments, as by the end of their five year apprenticeship they were expected to be experts, but if they worked hard they were promised a job at the end, which was more than many could expect.

Belfast in the 1880s was a rapidly expanding city. Between 1850 and 1901 its population increased from 90,000 to 350,000. The elegant Georgian homes in the centre were being replaced with Victorian commercial buildings as the middle and professional classes started to move to the outskirts. Linen mills, ship builders, and associated businesses provided employment not only for the working class, but also for the growing middle-class who had disposable income to spend in department stores such as that owned by Robinson, Ledlie and Ferguson. Many of the names that would be recognizable to anyone who shopped in Belfast before the 1990s were beginning their business careers around this time and a fellow apprentice of Crawford's was a boy called Tom Brand, later the owner of Brand & Co, which would become Brands and Norman.

To provide himself with some spending money, Crawford got a second job selling copies of the *Belfast Telegraph* outside the Great Northern Railway Station and later at Gibson's Corner in Castle Place. He saved some of the money earned, but spent the rest enjoying himself with his friends at some of the theatres or visiting circuses and fairs. He was a gregarious boy, and always made a point of learning and using the names of his regular customers, a practice that was often rewarded with an extra penny.

At the end of his apprenticeship Crawford was offered a position in the shop as an assistant manager at the salary of £25 per year, plus board and lodgings. It was more than many working-men in the city earned, but after two years he decided that it was time to move

Sir Crawford McCullagh

on. In 1889, he started working at John Hanna's drapery shop at 38 High Street, just down the road from the Bank Buildings. It was a thriving business, although considerably smaller than his former workplace, and meant more responsibility and more money. A few month's after starting in his new job he was on the move again, next door to John Porter's drapery shop at 34-36 High Street. He started as a buyer for their dress department, but his knack for business was immediately apparent and John Porter was so impressed that he increased his salary to £50, and promised that he would take over as General Manager when Porter himself retired.

The extra money was very welcome as he had recently become engaged to his landlord's daughter, Mary (Minnie) McCully. It was quite a long engagement and they would take long walks together to see the lovely new mansions that were being built on the outskirts of the city and make plans for their future. With the increase in his salary and promise of future promotion, Crawford and Minnie decided that they could afford to get married and so on 7 April 1890 they started their lives together. Sadly their happiness was to be short-lived. They had rented a house in the new development at Stranmillis and were delighted when Minnie became pregnant. Unfortunately the pregnancy was dogged by ill-health and when a son was born in January 1891 he only survived for a few days. Infant mortality was still high at this time and the young couple comforted themselves that they were both young and had plenty of time to have more children. Sadly it was not to be as, while they were still processing the loss of their firstborn, Minnie was diagnosed with tuberculosis.

At that time there was no cure for tuberculosis, but with a good diet and plenty of rest Minnie seemed to recover and was delighted to discover that she was pregnant again. But happiness was not to be their lot for on 26 October 1893, she died in the arms of her beloved Crawford, having given birth to a daughter a few days ear-

Famous Folk from Belfast

lier. Sadly the little girl did not survive long and died the next day. Minnie was only twenty-one.

As if this was not enough grief for Crawford to bear, his brother Samuel died from appendicitis just four months later. Crawford was just twenty-five and was all alone in the empty house in Stranmillis. He had money in the bank, but no-one with whom to share it and little reason to stay in Belfast so he started to look for positions in South Africa, a colony that was attracting a lot of men and women wanting to escape from Ireland.

It was when he was at his lowest ebb, one Saturday night walking down High Street, that he bumped into one of his old *Belfast Telegraph* customers, William Gibson.

William Gibson was a self-made man and a very successful one at that[3], he owned the largest and most successful jewellery company in the Empire and was also a philanthropist. The older man had been impressed by the young apprentice selling the paper outside his Belfast shop who had learnt his name and always had a cheery greeting. He had kept an eye on his progress through his various jobs and so he was alarmed to see how downcast and depressed Crawford looked. Crawford explained what had happened to him and that he was thinking about emigrating to South Africa.

Anxious to try to persuade the young man to reconsider, Gibson pointed out that there was a shop to let on the corner of High Street and Bridge Street and that he should consider opening up his own business. Crawford told him that he just had enough money to buy a one-way ticket to Cape Town with a little left over

---

3. Born in 1838 William Gibson was a jeweller by trade and like Crawford was a farmer's son. He had opened his first jewellers shop in North Street, before expanding to Castle Junction. He specialised in high quality silver and gold objects, and exhibited in America and Paris. He opened a branch of his business in Regent Street, London, later renamed the Goldsmith and Silversmith Co. When he died in 1913 he left a personal fortune of £305,601, or £35,000,000 in today's money.

Sir Crawford McCullagh

for spending, and made his farewell. He thought no more about it but on the following Monday Gibson walked into Porter's and handed Crawford a receipt for £125. He had bought the lease and fixtures and fittings of the shop and told a stunned Crawford to pay him back when he was able. It was the start of a long, successful business career that would literally change the shape of the city centre.

Just as he had impressed William Gibson, so too had he impressed the various agents that he had encountered both at the Bank Buildings and Porters. When he went to London to buy stock for his new shop from a wholesaler, he met one of these men, who guaranteed his credit, thus meaning that he was able to buy more stock than he had intended, and on credit rather than cash. It was just the start that he needed, and in later life he would always try to help anyone in the same position.

'C. McCullagh Millinery, Dress, Mantle and Ladies' General Outfitting' opened at 28 High Street in 1894. From the beginning he was determined to offer the ladies of Belfast a different shopping experience. He was offering good quality clothes, in the latest designs, in a range of colours and for an affordable price. Every lady who crossed the threshold was treated the same. When he was on his buying trips to London he read the latest magazines and strolled along looking in the windows of the exclusive shops, so that he could stay ahead of the fashion trends.

McCullagh's was soon one of *the* places to shop for the fashionable middleclass ladies of Belfast. There was a personal touch, with regular clientele always addressed by name. Belfast at this time had a growing middleclass, with the wives and daughters of managers and junior directors wanting to be dressed in the latest fashion, but without the resources to buy designer originals. McCullagh's offered affordable, well-made fashion. Nor did Crawford confine himself to selling other people's designs. A trip to Portrush, dur-

Famous Folk from Belfast

ing which he saw a Guard's band, led to him designing a feminine version of the Guard's jacket, which proved very popular among the ladies of Belfast. Other designs were to follow and soon he started manufacturing coats under the name 'The Belfast Coat and Costume Company'.

As his business prospered and grew he moved to larger premises at 15-17 High Street and advertised in the *News Letter* for a draper's assistant. He was to get more than he bargained. Maggie Brodie was 25 years old and was very attractive. She had left school at 16 and gone to serve an apprenticeship at her uncle's cotton manufacturing company outside Manchester. She stood out from all the other applicants and was taken on for a salary of £12. Soon she was making her mark on the shop floor, rearranging the layout, adding little touches of decoration and staying behind after hours to complete her latest project, or to help Crawford with his accounting books. Soon they were spending more and more time with each other outside the shop, day-trips to Bangor, trips to the theatre and on 26 July 1897, at Fortwilliam Presbyterian Church, Maggie Brodie became Mrs Crawford McCullagh.

Crawford and Maggie's marriage was a very unusual one for their class and at the end of the nineteenth century. Upon marriage it was usual for women to give up their jobs. In fact, usually there wasn't a choice as many firms and public bodies refused to employ married women, only single women and widows. If a woman was able to retain her job after her marriage, then the arrival of children would mean that she had to stay at home. Maggie did not see why she should, and Crawford agreed. They had moved to a house in Helen's Bay, commuting in each day by train, and when their children started to arrive they simply employed a nanny. For Crawford, Maggie was too valuable to stay at home – she was a better manager than she was a cook and he could afford to hire domestic staff. Throughout their marriage they were very much

Sir Crawford McCullagh

a team, he always called her *'my best pal'*, and she was as much a workaholic as him.

Their first daughter, Helen, was born in 1900 and was followed by a second daughter, Margaret Eileen [Daisy] in 1903, and a son Joseph Crawford McCullagh in 1907. While they were undoubtedly loved and cherished, they took second place in their parents' lives; the most important people in Crawford and Maggie's lives were each other.

The move to Helen's Bay had another, unlooked for but nevertheless profitable and advantageous side effect. Crawford and Maggie were both committed Presbyterians and so joined the local congregation and soon became active members. Soon Crawford was elected to the Church Committee, where his fellow committee members included some of the most influential industrialists, professionals and fellow merchants in Belfast. They included Thomas Workman, the ship-builder, James Mackie, of James Mackie and Sons Ltd and the High Sheriff of Co. Down, George Herbert Brown. Crawford was appointed as Treasurer between 1900 and 1908, and was then elected as an Elder in 1911. He and Maggie were now moving in the same social circles as some of the most influential families in the city.

William Gibson had continued to keep a paternal eye on his protégé. By 1903, Crawford had decided that he should expand his business into a department store, but there wasn't a suitable site available. Talking his plans over with his mentor, Gibson said that he would lease him a block of old-style shops on the south side of Castle Place and allow him to redevelop the site. In 1904 he suggested to Crawford that it might be an idea to make a visit to America and Canada to see the large department stores in the main cities. The plan was to spend a few days in New York, visiting Macy's, Bloomindales etc and then travelling to Toronto, where Gibson had arranged for him to stay with his friend Timothy

Famous Folk from Belfast

Eaton[4], owner of T. Eaton & Co. the largest department store and mail-order catalogue business in Canada. The Eaton's proved to be very generous hosts and arranged daily visits to their Toronto store, where Crawford was shown every aspect of the business, from the overhead pneumatic tubes carrying cash to and from the counters, through the lifts and lighting, to the range and arrangement of stock. He was inspired and returned home brimming with ideas.

The resulting building is still there, and recent renovations also uncovered the original signage. Castle Buildings was built in two phases, with the first opening on 6 May 1905. It was impossibly glamorous and every bit as elegant and impressive as any London store. An uniformed doorman opened the impressive polished mahogany doors to admit the customer to two floors of goods, displayed in a sea of gleaming glass, marble and polished brass. A magnificent staircase swept the customer up to more delights on the first floor. The first pneumatic tube system in Ireland whizzed the payments to and from the counter, where elegant sales assistants tended to your every need.

The same year as Crawford opened his new department store, he was persuaded by his friends and fellow Helen's Bay congregants to run for election to the City Council. This made a great deal of sense. His development at 12-18 Castle Place had a rateable value of £1,400 [£168,816.22 today] making him the largest rate payer in the centre of the city. He put his name forward for the vacant Cromac Ward and was unopposed. Thus started a connection with the City Council that was to last for almost the rest of his life.

---

4. Timothy Eaton was born in Clogher, Co. Antrim [no this is not a typo] in 1834 so was a contemporary of Gibsons. He was orphaned at the age of 14 and at the age of 20 emigrated to Canada with his brother James. They opened a dry goods shop in Fish Creek, St Mary's but, following his marriage and a quarrel, Timothy and his wife moved to Toronto where they opened a new shop. The business prospered and then, in 1884, they branched out into a mail-order catalogue. By the time of Crawford's visit the catalogue was published twice a year and ran to over 400 pages.

Sir Crawford McCullagh

The City Council was, at the time of his election, housed in the old Town Hall on Victoria Street[5]. The city status had only been awarded around two decades earlier, in 1888, and the city fathers were struggling to keep up to date with the municipal needs of a thriving centre of commerce and industry. This would have been difficult enough in any city of a comparable size with the competing social and commercial factions, but politics in Belfast was complicated further by the sectarian nature of life in the city, with powerful voices off-stage, trying to keep a lid on the demands of the workers by emphasizing their sectarian differences. Crawford was a Unionist, and he made no apologies for that. He felt that the prosperity of his adopted city depended on its continuing membership of the wider economic market that the Union ensured. It wasn't just that there was an economic argument to be made to maintain the political union with the rest of the United Kingdom, that political union meant that Ireland was an integral part of the British Empire – and her markets, rather than exiting to go it alone. This did not mean that he was sectarian. In fact one of his closest friends was the nationalist 'Wee' Joe Devlin[6]. He was determined to use his voice on the council to improve the status of the city and also improve the lives of all the citizens.

In 1908 he was given a chance to improve the housing in the city when he was appointed Chairman of the Improvement Committee. Housing for the poorest in the city was a disgrace. If you have time look for the photographs of A. R. Hogg, held by the Ulster Museum, who was employed by the council to take photographs

---

5. Construction of the new City Hall, on the site of the old Linen Hall, started in 1898. It was completed in 1906.

6. Joseph Devlin, 1871-1934, was a nationalist politican and journalist. He was the MP for Belfast West between 1908 and 1922, even defeating Eamon De Valera in the 1918 election. He supported both Redmond and Dillon in the Parliamentary Party. He was a nationalist rather than a republican and supported the partition as he had been led to believe that it was only a temporary solution by Lloyd George.

of the living conditions in the city. As people poured into the city in search of work, the age old problem of accommodation became more acute. Overcrowding and poor sanitation all contributed to a health hazard with high rates of infant mortality, regular outbreaks of typhus, and as Crawford knew from personal experience perfect breeding conditions for tuberculousis. This was not to say that Crawford was the first person on the council to want to improve living conditions. Various projects had been proposed and implemented, especially in the second half of the nineteenth century. One scheme to improve sanitation resulted in women being admitted to vote in council elections, thanks to the efforts of Isabella Tod, the first women in Ireland to be able to vote. Industrialists often provided housing for their workforce and there were philanthropic housing developments. Conditions were improving but there was still plenty to do. The Committee approved the demolition of seven hundred slum dwellings[7] in the Millfield area to be replaced by terraced, 'parlour' homes, with outside dry closets [toilet] in a back yard, shuttered front windows, foot-scrappers at the front door, and a gas light and gas cooking ring.

At the same time as he was improving housing in the poorest areas of the city he was also involved in property development with his good friend Jo Jo McConnell, son of Robert McConnell, a former Lord Mayor and major property developer in the ever expanding city. Crawford was one of his major investors and together they pursued their dream of affordable housing in beautiful surroundings. They were very much influenced by Ebenezer Howard, the father of the garden city movement.

By the 1911, Crawford had been elected High Sheriff of Belfast and it was in this role that he and Maggie attended the launch of the *Titanic* on 31 May. He had joined the Ulster Unionist Council

---

7. Often these dwellings were rat and damp infested rooms, with no ventilation or sanitation.

Sir Crawford McCullagh

and although not actively involved in it certainly knew about the gun-running plans prior to Fred Crawford setting off to Germany. If he felt any qualms about this he certainly didn't share them. Nor did he appear to have any problem being friends with both Edward Carson and Lord Pirrie, one a Unionist and the other a supporter of Home Rule. On the 28 September 1912, in his capacity as High Sheriff of Belfast, he welcomed Edward Carson, James Craig and the rest of the Unionist leaders to the City Hall, where they signed the Ulster Covenant. As Ireland looked as if it was about to descend into a civil war, with rival armed paramilitary groups openly parading and training, in April 1914 Crawford was elected Lord Mayor of Belfast. A few months later the country was at war and the majority of the Irishmen who had been preparing to defend their communities, instead went to the killing fields of France.

Crawford, with Margaret (as she was now calling herself) by his side threw themselves into the war effort. When, on 8 May 1915 the 36th Ulster Division paraded through the streets of Belfast, prior to departing on troop ships for the Front, Crawford and Margaret were there to see them off. They worked tirelessly raising money for hospital equipment and beds, hosting receptions for the wounded or visiting troops. So tireless was he that he appeared to be chairing every major civic or philanthropic venture during the war. He was re-elected, unopposed, not just in 1915 but also in 1916 and 1917. All his hard work did not go unrewarded and on 16 May 1915 he was awarded a knighthood in a ceremony attended by the Lord Lieutenant of Ireland, Lord Wimborne, for services to the War Effort.

Of course, at this distance it is possible to criticize some of his actions during the war, such as when he did nothing to protect a former Lord Mayor, Sir Otto Jaffa, who was hounded out of public

Famous Folk from Belfast

office due to being born in Germany[8] in the wake of the sinking of the *Lusitania* and a year later he chaired the inaugural meeting of the Belfast Anti-German Union[9].

In the midst of all his civic responsibilities, in 1915, Sir Crawford realised a long held dream. When he was a young apprentice and later when he was courting Maggie, he used to take walks along the coast at Whiteabbey and look at the large 'Merchant Prince' houses on the coast. One in particular had seized his imagination. Designed by Charles Lanyon, Lismara had been built in 1850 for a flax merchant, John Finlay. It had passed through a number of hands, including Lanyon's son Herbert, but in 1915 the current owner, Major Harold Robinson (of Robinson and Cleaver department store) decided to sell and Sir Crawford snapped it up.

Of all his activities during the First World War the most important, and the one for which he should have received more recognition, was the Silence in remembrance of the dead. The Battle of the Somme, which started on 1 July 1916, had a devastating effect on the people of Belfast and farther afield. The 36th Ulster Division was in the front line, and suffered horrific and unimaginable losses. In the first thirty-six hours of the attack the casualty list ran to 5,500. It was calculated later that there was hardly a town or townland in the counties from which the soldiers came that had not received a telegram informing them of death or injury. In Belfast that could be translated to hardly any street. The death and destruction was

---

8. Sir Otto Jaffe was twice Lord Mayor of Belfast. Despite his son and nephew both serving in the British Army, he was accused of being a German spy and, describing himself as being *'overwhelmed with pain and sorrow'* he wrote to the *Northern Whig* that *"how anyone who has any knowledge of me and my life would think that I could approve of the horrible and detestable actions of which she (Germany) has been guilty is almost beyond my comprehension."*

9. However, with regard to the latter it was actually a gathering of industrialists who wanted to try to protect their position with a Customs Union.

SIR CRAWFORD MCCULLAGH

indiscriminate: it didn't matter if you were from the Shankhill or the Falls, from wealth or poverty, Catholic, Protestant or Jew.

Obviously something had to be done to recognize the pain and the loss. The Orange Order had cancelled its annual 12 July demonstrations. This inspired Sir Crawford to ask that all businesses be suspended for five minutes[10] from 12 noon on the 12th, to remember the dead, he also asked that traffic should stop and blinds lowered in public buildings and private homes. The response was amazing. For five minutes the whole city stopped in its tracks, trains halted, people stood with heads bowed and remembered not only the dead of the Somme, but also the other battles fought.

Sir Crawford's three years as Lord Mayor officially ended in January 1917, although he remained in the Council Chamber and it did not signal an end to his involvement in politics. He was invited to join the Irish Convention, which was established by Lloyd George to try to produce some workable solution to the Home Rule question. While for those in England, Scotland and Wales the signing of the armistice meant a return to normality, for the people on the island of Ireland it meant a period of great political unrest. The question of Home Rule, which had been shelved for the duration of the war, had been further complicated by the reaction to the execution of the leaders of the Easter Rising. Sinn Fein was now posing a credible threat, not only to the nationalist Irish Parliamentary Party, but also to Unionist politicians. I do not propose to go into the whole story here, because most people know the history and indeed we are still living the history today.

---

10. While the credit for the two-minute silence is often, erroneously, attributed to Sir Crawford, he was certainly the first elected official to request a period of silence in remembrance for the fallen. The credit lies with the Mayor of Cape Town, Sir Harry Hands who ordered a two minute silence after the firing of the noon-day gun every day for a year (1918-1919) to remember the dead.

Famous Folk from Belfast

The Municipal elections in 1920 saw Sinn Fein councilors returned to the council for the first time and the Government of Ireland Bill divided the country into two separate states. As a member of the Ulster Unionist Council, Sir Crawford was privy to all the discussions taking place at the time, while as a member of the Irish Convention he tried to maintain links with politicians throughout the island.

While all of this political uncertainty, with the concurrent civil unrest [riots, shootings, murders etc] was going on Sir Crawford was still, first and foremost, a businessman anxious to maintain the economic success he had enjoyed thus far, and on which so many jobs depended. He was also a proud father to his children and in 1921 was delighted when his eldest daughter, Helen, was married to Andrew Wilson. His other daughter Daisy, proved to be slightly more troublesome as she launched herself on the 'flapper' social scene in the London, drinking cocktails and dancing to dawn with the other 'bright young things'. One can imagine the horror with which her tea-total parents viewed her activities and sigh of relief they must have heaved when she announced her engagement to Victor Henderson in 1922. Their son, 'Boysie', had completed his education at Campbell College in 1924 and had joined the family business, but his abiding passion in life was for ornithology and he became one of the leading Ornithologists in the country, leaving a legacy to the Belfast Zoo which named a birdhouse in his memory.

Ever ahead of the trends, Sir Crawford now branched out into public entertainment. The war had seen an increase in interest in the new technology of moving pictures, and he had been in love with the 'silver screen' since a visit in 1910 to the Electric Cinema in York Street. While his cinema was not the first, or even one of the first cinemas in Belfast it was certainly the most luxurious. The Classic Cinema was on the site of the old Castle Market. The grand

SIR CRAWFORD MCCULLAGH

auditorium could seat 1,804 who, on the opening (on Christmas Eve 1923), were treated to a 30 piece orchestra accompanying the silent film *Chu-Chin-Chow*. The interior of the cinema was the last word in sophistication with a black and gold colour scheme. In her biography of her great grandfather, Susan Cunningham paints the scene:

> *'The cinema manager, Mr Noel Hobart, always in full evening dress, stood at the top of the steps leading from the semi circular main entrance and presided over immaculately presented usherettes who were trained to the highest standards. The same black and gold colour scheme was used in the design of the staff uniforms with the usherettes wearing trouser suits.'*

In a city torn by civil unrest, economic uncertainty, strikes and still coming to terms with the grief of so many lives lost or destroyed during four years of war and the subsequent Spanish flu epidemic, the Classic provided a touch of glamour. You could even dine before the film in an elegant restaurant, with linen table cloths and silver service. As with so many of Sir Crawford's business ventures the cinema provided affordable luxury for everyone, with the same deference being shown to the young couple on their only 'treat' in months as the fur-wrapped couple in evening dress. He understood the need to escape from reality, if only for a couple of hours.

In 1931, Sir Crawford was again elected Lord Mayor and in his inaugural speech reminded his fellow council members that they were there to serve all the people of the city,

> *"no matter what political affiliation'* and *'if each kept this in mind, their deliberations would be more harmonious and the honour and prestige of their beloved city enhanced."*

While it is always tempting to whitewash the subject of any biography, I must also record that it was at this time that he developed the 'City Hall Party' which monopolized all offices within the control of the ruling party. No matter what the intention may have been the result was that for the next decades all offices within the council were monopolized by the Unionist party, not all of whom were as civic minded as Sir Crawford.

In the wake of the Wall Street Crash of 1929, industry in Northern Ireland as elsewhere in the world, was almost on its knees. Almost half the insured[11] workers in shipbuilding and engineering and a third in the linen industry were unemployed. Despite the best efforts of the trade union movement [see Winnie Carney], there were tens of thousands of women workers who were not insured and therefore ineligible for support. For those without insurance unemployment resulted in total destitution. Belfast still operated on a system of Outdoor Relief administered by the Board of Guardians. Relief was only given when all savings had been exhausted, and then only in the form of grocery chits. The Union Workhouse, still operating on the Lisburn Road, was not able to admit all those who qualified for admission. Nor was the age-old tradition of emigration an option, as the traditional destinations, America, Canada and Australia, were also combating mass unemployment and, in the case of America, were actually sending non-naturalised immigrants back to their country of origin. On 3 October 1932, in a rare moment of sectarian unity, there was a demonstration of around 60,000 men and women protesting the situation at the Customs House, organized by the trade union movement. Over the next week there were targeted protests at the Union Workhouse with protesters lying on tramlines to block the road and, inevitably, rioting broke out. A curfew was declared and the police sent in to break down barricades and protest meetings in both communities. Despite the efforts of some to divide the protesters along traditional sectarian lines, the leaders stayed

---

11. A form of National Insurance had been introduced before the war, see the chapter on Winnie Carney for more information.

SIR CRAWFORD MCCULLAGH

united and refused to be swayed. Alarmed by the situation Sir Crawford met with the Board of Guardians and a new range of relief schemes was agreed, while at the same time they applied pressure to the new Government in Stormont to do the same. Over the next years Belfast Corporation spent more than £4,000 weekly on outdoor relief, and provided employment by starting a number of civic improvement schemes such as the construction of the Lagan Embankment, drainage schemes and housing.

One such scheme was the construction of the Belfast Zoo. The Corporation-run pleasure grounds at Bellevue had been a popular destination for daytrippers and they now had the opportunity to develop over 12 additional acres up the side of the Cavehill as a zoo. This gave employment to around 150 men and Sir Crawford opened the new Bellevue Zoo on 28 March 1934. The development of the site continued and in May 1936, Sir Crawford was delighted to open the Floral Hall saying in his opening address that:

> '...[He] hoped that the Corporation could make it a paying proposition ... [but] it was his and his colleagues belief that a great city of Belfast could not count everything in pounds, shilling and pence.'

He would be appalled by the state of the hall today.

Sir Crawford's dedication to promoting Belfast and determination that all should benefit meant that even the Nationalist councillors were prepared to nominate and vote for him to remain in his position as Lord Mayor from 1931 to 1942. A large part of the role of Lord Mayor was civic entertaining and Sir Crawford and Lady McCullagh threw themselves into this with great gusto. However, unlike many of his predecessors and successors, this entertainment didn't cost the ratepayers any money as he financed it himself, to the cost of £5,000 [today £350,000] per year. Over the years he welcomed royalty and ratepayers with the same generosity. Visiting dignitaries would often be treated to dinner at Lismara, and charities were also offered the grounds of his home as the venue for fund-raising garden parties or fetes. As Lord Mayor of Belfast, Sir Crawford and Margaret travelled to represent the city at major events including the coronation of George VI in 1937.

Ever aware of the advantages of advertisement, Sir Crawford was determined to use the media to gain as much good publicity for his city as possible. He courted the newspapers, throughout Ireland and the UK, and was a frequent visitor to public events at which he made sure that he was photographed by the prominent people of the day. Despite his efforts, he was not always recognised, even at home. He delighted in telling about one such occasion:

> '*I went into a certain establishment to buy an outside easy chair for my daughter Helen … and after succeeding in getting what I wanted I paid for the chair and told the assistant I would send the car round for it. She asked me what name and when I said the Lord Mayor she said, 'Oh, go on with you, none of that now!' I said, 'But I am the Lord Mayor', but I'm afraid I did not succeed in convincing her, she thought I was making fun of her.*'

In 1939, the world was once more at war and Sir Crawford was once more trying to guide his city through difficult times. He and Margaret threw themselves into the war effort, reviving many of the relief organisations they had supported in the 1914-18 war. There was one vital difference, as the advances in aviation meant that there was a real danger that Belfast would be within the range of the Luftwaffe bombers. Sir Crawford drove the construction of public air-raid shelters and made plans for the evacuation of the city. However he and the Corporation were limited in what they could actually do, as civil defence was a government matter, and the government appeared to be complacent and wrong-footed. Belfast was left with only twenty-two anti-aircraft guns and no searchlights. It was as if the idea that the city as a whole would be a target hadn't crossed their minds. Despite this the Corporation did

Sir Crawford McCullagh

manage to build around 200 public shelters, although they were to prove inadequate in the scale of the raids.

When the Belfast Blitz started in April 1941 the city was devastated. The shipyard, docks and aircraft factories were the main target but there was hardly an area of the city that was not touched. There were four raids in total. The first was an exploratory one to test the city's defences, which were very poor. On the second night, Easter Tuesday, 15 April 1941, 200 bombers attacked the city, dropping high explosive bombs at the main industrial areas, resulting in 900 deaths and 1,500 injuries. Apart from London this was the highest loss of life in any night raid during the blitz, including Coventry. The third raid was on 4th May, resulting in 150 deaths but greater destruction of property as wave after wave of incendiary bombs were dropped causing fire-storms. Unable to cope, the head of the fire-service phoned his opposite number in Dublin begging for help and fire-fighters and their engines came from Dublin, Dun Laoghaire, Drogheda and Dundalk, fighting alongside their Belfast colleagues for over three days to try to contain the fires. The final raid, the following night, continued to rain down incendiary devices.

Sir Crawford toured the city, trying to come to terms with the extent of the devastation. By the time of the last attack in May over 3,200 houses were completely destroyed, almost 4,000 seriously damaged and a further 50,000 still habitable but in need of extensive repair. Thousands had fled the city into the countryside, although many returned each day to try to pick up the pieces of the city's commercial, construction and business life.

He was now 74, and had given over three decades of service to his adopted city, many of them as Lord Mayor. While still in robust good health himself, Margaret was being to suffer from ill-health. He felt that it was the right time to hand over the role of first citizen to a younger man, with more energy for the massive task at hand. Accordingly, he informed his fellow councilors that he would not accept nomination for the role in 1942. The plan was to step back and enjoy a well-earned rest. But the best laid plans etc… His replacement, Alderman George R Black, almost immediately started to suffer from ill-health and died in December 1942. Sir Crawford was prevailed upon to step back into public life and assume the title of Lord Mayor for the remainder of the mayoral year, and was then unanimously re-elected for 1943-44, his sixteenth term in office.

The start of 1944 saw great personal sadness for Sir Crawford, as his beloved 'best pal' Margaret finally succumbed to stomach cancer. Her role as Lady Mayoress had been taken over by her daughters in recent years, as her health had started to fail, but her position as the centre of the family had not been altered. Sir Crawford always paid tribute to her role in his success. She may have found the role of first lady of the city difficult at first, being naturally shy, but she had overcome her fears and her lack of 'airs' had worked to her advantage as she chaired meetings to raise money for the various charities closest to her heart. She was very much an equal partner in the marriage at a time when this was unusual. Sir Crawford always consulted her before going ahead with a new business venture, and valued her advice. Together, they struggled to understand and support their children, two of whom struggled with alcohol dependence, despite their own avowed teetotal abstinence. They were both guided by their devout and practical Christian faith to try to help those less fortunate than themselves. Her death left a huge gap in his public and private life.

When the American army arrived in Belfast, in preparation for the D Day landings, Sir Crawford had worked to make their stay as pleasant as possible, urging everyone to be welcoming to their American 'cousins'. It was as Lord Mayor that he was able to celebrate the end of the war in Europe and against Japan. He requested

Sir Crawford McCullagh

that all places of public entertainment should be kept open, past normal opening hours and officiated at the public celebrations. On 24 August 1945 the Supreme Commander of the American Forces, Dwight D. Eisenhower arrived in Belfast to thank the Lord Mayor and the citizens of Belfast for their:

> *'surrender to them during 1942 and 1943 of their homes and hearts.'*

As was his custom, Sir Crawford invited General Eisenhower to stay at Lismara and held a special dinner in his honour. By now an old man, Sir Crawford had retired to bed shortly after midnight, but his daughter Daisy stayed up drinking with the General into the *'wee small hours'*. A photograph of the house party taken the next morning shows a refreshed looking Sir Crawford beaming at the camera beside a rather under-power General and Daisy.

At the end of the war Belfast was still recovering from the physical damage of the Blitz, let alone the emotional damage of so much loss of life and injury. Sir Crawford had instituted a Citizen's Fund, run by the council to provide financial help for those who had lost everything and the council had set about replacing and repairing the damage to the housing stock. However he recognised that it was time to step aside and let a younger generation take over. He was also, increasingly, suffering from bouts of ill-health and so announced that he was going to retire from public life. His decision to retire was commemorated by an editorial in the *Belfast Telegraph* that said:

> *'In large measure Belfast is a self-made city owing more to the industry of its inhabitants than to anything else. Sir Crawford's career has been typical of this fundamental characteristic and he had shown those qualities that we like to think are representative of the Ulsterman – industrious, common sense, humour and generosity ... Here was a man who wore his honours well, and who could always*

Famous Folk from Belfast

be counted on to discharge the duties of his office with a natural sense of the fitness of things.'

Sir Crawford died on 13 April 1948 at his home, Lismara.

Even leaving aside the fact that he was the longest serving Lord Mayor in Belfast, and possibly in Ireland, Sir Crawford deserves his place in a book about the history of Belfast. As much, if not more than anyone else in the opening decades of the twentieth century he shaped the physical city, from shopping arcades, department stores and places of entertainment to civic buildings and public housing. A large part of his economic success was that he never lost touch with what the public wanted. He insisted that every customer who set foot in his shops or cinemas was treated with the same level of respect and welcome, no matter who or what they were. This was translated into his public life. He saw himself as the Lord Mayor of every citizen of Belfast and tried to make the city he loved a better place for everyone. Of course he made mistakes, but in general he was a unifying force in a divided council chamber. He never forgot that he had achieved his first step to success through the generosity of another, and always tried to pay it forward. One of his last acts as Lord Mayor was to launch the Shilling Fund to reward the bravery of James Magennis VC. His intention was not to deny a Catholic official civic recognition, but rather to give a young naval rating a financially secure future.

No matter that he became one of the 'Merchant Princes', he never forgot that he had once been the penniless apprentice selling the *Belfast Telegraph* on Gibson's corner.

No Mean City: Men and Women who Built Belfast

Human building blocks of a City

Newspaper proprietors, Linen barons, factory owners, engineers mill workers and labourers.

In little over one hundred and fifty years Belfast went from a small market town of around 8000 inhabitants to one of the industrial centres of the world with a population approaching 400,000. It was known as Linenopolis and the manufacturing of linen, ships and associated industries drove the economy of not only the city, but also the north east of Ireland. To fully acknowledge the many industrialists who played a part in that growth would require several volumes. As such I have limited myself to selecting examples from the key sectors of industry which drove Belfast's extraordinary rise to pre-eminence as one of Britain's [and thus at that time, the world's] leading industrial centres.

Francis Joy and family

Francis Joy was born in Killead, Co. Antrim in 1697. As a young man he moved to Belfast to practice as a lawyer and married

Famous Folk from Belfast

Margaret Martin, whose grandfather George had been Sovereign of Belfast. They had three children, Henry, Robert and Ann, all of whom were to help shape the growing town. In 1737, as a result of a bad debt he found himself the proud owner of a small printing business and rather than selling it on decided to start up a newspaper with the full title of *The Belfast News-Letter and General Advertiser*. Shortly after he started publishing the *Newsletter* there was a paper shortage so he opened up a paper mill and placed strong paper bags in towns and villages for donations of rags, used in paper making. He soon dominated paper making in Ireland. As he grew more prosperous he moved to Randalstown but kept in close contact with his sons and daughter who remained in Belfast. Like his granddaughter Mary Ann McCracken he lived into his nineties.

When their father left Belfast Henry Joy was twenty-five and Robert[1] was twenty-three and they were left in charge of both the law practice and the *Newsletter*. By 1797 they built a paper mill at Cromac. During the 1770s there was great rural distress due to poor harvests and lack of traditional work such as hand-loom weaving, which led to people arriving in search of either work or a sea passage in Belfast. In a response to the obvious destitution the Belfast Charitable Society was set up in 1752 and by 1767 they had raised enough money to start building the Poor House. Both Joy brothers were leading members of the Society and when a lottery was established to raise money they were printed and distributed by H & R Joy. Robert Joy actually designed the Poorhouse, and his vision is still here for us to enjoy today, with some additions.

---

1. When Robert was arranging his marriage to Grizell Rainey of Magherafelt in 1751, he sent her a letter assuring her that 'Mr Rankin has consented to oblige me, provided it be done with secrecy.' A reminder that marriages solemnized by Presbyterians were illegal until the early nineteenth century.

The Men and Women who Built Belfast

In 1778 the Belfast Charitable Committee decided to provide employment for the young children in their care by setting up a cotton spinning operation. In 1779 Robert and his friend Thomas McCabe, at their own expense, installed a spinning jenny in the Poorhouse to train the young boys so that they could be employed once they had left their care, they also paid the children and made sure that they did not work long hours, an unheard of level of concern in an age when young boys were still being sent up chimneys. In 1784 Robert and Thomas, joined by Ann's husband John McCracken, set up the first cotton mill in Ireland. It was the start of a cotton industry in Belfast. By 1790 it was estimated that there were up to eight thousand people employed in the industry in the town and outlying districts.

Both Henry and Robert were founding members of the 1st Belfast Volunteer Company along with their nephew Francis McCracken, the oldest brother of Henry Joy and Mary Ann McCracken. Henry McCracken was also a founding member of the Belfast Chamber of Commerce in 1783 which petitioned the Irish House of Commons for assistance in redeveloping the harbour with *a straight cut which would for ever be kept open by the Waters of the River Lagan running therin'* which was the foundation of what became one of the largest ports in Ireland. As the 'deputy'[2] Town Clerk of Belfast from 1759 to 1772 he helped to develop the commercial life of the town, and even after relinquishing the office was the driving force behind the building of the White Linenhall in 1783.

As I comment in another chapter there were a confusing embarrassment of Henry Joys, leaving aside the Henry Joy McCracken of United Irishmen fame. Both Robert and Henry had sons called Henry Joy. Robert's son Henry, known as Henry Joy jnr took over

---

2. As a Presbyterian he was forbidden by the Test Act from holding any public office, however he could be a 'deputy'. This meant that the letter of the law was adhered to, while he was in fact the actual Town Clerk.

as editor and proprietor of the *News-Letter* which he sold in 1795, while Henry's son Henry, known as Counsellor Joy, became Chief Baron of the Irish Court of Exchequer in Dublin. When Mary Ann McCracken was visiting her brother in Kilmainham jail he provided her with professional help and a safe place to stay.

Ann Joy was the baby of the family and her older brothers were very close to her, both emotionally and physically, as their houses were side by side in High Street in the early days of her marriage. She had remained in Belfast with them when their father had moved to Randalstown but was not content to merely keep house for her brothers while waiting for a suitable husband. She opened a small milliner's shop in High Street, and when she married Captain John McCracken she sold the shop but started up a muslin business. This was very unusual in the eighteenth century so it is not surprising that all of her children should show such independent spirits. Once when her two eldest children were still young she accompanied her husband to Liverpool, leaving them in the care of their paternal grandmother. She decided to travel home alone and, just off Ballywalter, the ship was wrecked and they had to wade ashore from a small 'lifeboat'. It would have been difficult enough to achieve in the long skirts and cloaks that ladies wore but she was further encumbered by 200 golden guineas sewn into her clothing that she was carrying for John.

Like her brothers she was actively involved in the Poorhouse and often took her children to visit. She was a loving support not only to her husband and children but also to the young Edward Bunting who she welcomed into her home. Driven by a profound faith she was also fully abreast with and largely sympathetic to all the latest radical ideas. Given that her husband was away for long periods of time it can be assumed that it was she who decided to send her younger children to David Manson's school and it is known that she was an admirer of Thomas Paine, until he started to attack reli-

The Men and Women who Built Belfast

gion. Like Harry and Mary Ann she had a great faith in *'Providence that can bring good out of evil'*[3] and while we do not know that she supported the rebellion she certainly never reproached her children for their involvement, despite the anguish she felt at Harry's execution.

The Mulholland's York Street Flax Spinning Mill

In the opening decades of the nineteenth century cotton spinning was one of the main employers in the expanding town of Belfast. It was based largely in the Smithfield area, employing over 1,000 men, women and children.[4] In 1815 a 'dealer' called Thomas Mulholland[5] bought a five-story cotton mill in Winetavern Street. It proved a great success and his son, another Thomas, bought another one in Francis Street, and then built yet another in Henry Street in 1822, making him the leading textile manufacturer in Belfast.

This was the heyday of cotton production in Belfast however in 1824 two events occurred that were to change both Thomas jnr's life and also that of thousands of workers. The first was that the tariff barrier that had protected Irish cotton from direct competition from the rest of Britain was lifted and the second was that James Kay of Preston patented a wet spinning process for fine linen.

The first definite reference to an Irish Linen trade was in the 13th century when it was apparently flourishing in the abbeys in Bangor, Newtownards and Armagh, but it was largely domes-

---

3. A letter to Mary Ann dated 16 November 1796 when Mary Ann was in Dublin visiting Harry who was in Kilmainham jail.
4. By 1825 more than 3,500 were employed in around twenty mills in what would now be referred to as the greater Belfast area. By the 1840s the main centre for cotton production was centred in Ballymacarrett, with disastrous consequences for the inhabitants during the Great Famine.
5. Thomas was married to Ann Doe and when he bought two houses in 1803 he had signed the papers with an 'X'.

tic. By the middle of the eighteenth century linen was the most commonly produced textile in Ireland, and wearing it was seen as a source of patriotic pride for high society in Dublin during Grattan's Parliament. However production was largely a rural, domestic occupation. Flax was a particularly suitable cash crop for small holdings and could be spun and woven by the entire family. The finished 'brown' cloth was then sold to dealers for bleaching and exports, most of it through the port of Belfast. By 1785 the trade was so important to the growing town that a White Linen Hall was erected[6] but production still remained largely domestic.

Two further events helped to change Thomas's mind about remaining in cotton production. A recession in the cotton industry, starting around 1826, was followed by a fire in the Henry Street mill in 1828, which was totally destroyed. Rather than rebuilding a cotton mill he and his brothers Andrew and St Clair, together with their business partner John Hind, decided to travel to England to investigate flax spinning in the major textile centres of York and Leeds. They knew that large amounts of flax was being exported to England each year, to be spun and then returned to Ireland for weaving so recognised the gap in the market at home. They imported the idea to their remaining mill in Francis Street, installing 1,000 flax spindles and when this proved a success they rebuilt their Henry Street mill in 1830 with 8,000 flax spindles, it became known as the York Street Flax Spinning Mill. By 1856 there were 25,000 spindles and it was the largest mill of its kind in the world.

Andrew had married Elizabeth McDonnell in 1818 and had a son, John, and four daughters. As well as one of the town's leading businessmen he also served on the newly created council and was elected Mayor in 1845, just as the effects of the famine were

---

6. On the site of the current City Hall

The Men and Women who Built Belfast

beginning to be felt in Belfast. As will be discussed elsewhere, the full scale of the famine caught the civic authorities off-guard and was far beyond anything that had been experienced before. As it progressed and thousands of people flooded into Belfast in search of work, a boat or just food, the local authorities found themselves fire-fighting. Individuals tried to help and Andrew personally donated around £1,000 [£120,000] to various relief funds. He retired from the family business the following year, handing it over to his son John, who was later created Baron Dunleath. His philanthropy continued in his later years and it was he that donated the magnificent pipe organ to the Ulster Hall in 1862. The family connection to the York St Spinning Mill continued well into the twentieth century, when my mother worked as a designer in the firm in the late 1950s her much-loved boss was Sir Harry Mulholland.

William Dargan – civil engineer

Belfast's industrial entrepreneurs could only succeed if they could get their raw materials delivered to them and their finished products exported by sea. Efforts had been made to improve the docks at the end of High Street throughout the eighteenth century, but it was not until the 1840s that there was a large-scale redevelopment.

William Dargan was born in 1799 into a Carlow tenant farming family. Not much is known about his early life, but we do know that his first job was in England working in the offices of Thomas Telford[7], working on the construction of the Holyhead Road at the age of 21. Back in Ireland one of his first commissions was the main street in Banbridge, which is largely untouched today. He was closely involved in the construction of the Ulster Canal, which ran from Lough Erne to Belfast, as well as the Newry Canal.

---

7. Thomas Telford was a Scottish civil engineer who designed many of the major canals including the Caledonian and Ellesmere canals as well as the Menai Suspension Bridge.

Famous Folk from Belfast

In 1840 he was contracted by the Ballast Board[8] who had the right to purchase land and private docks to divert, deepen and direct the Lagan through money raised by port dues. Dargan intended to make two cuts to straighten and deepen the river and made his first cut in 1840, completed within a year. The dredged mud was dumped on the Co. Down side of the river, where the Queen's Bridge is now, and over the next 8 years the dredged 'spoil' formed an area around 59 acres. In straightening the river he had created an island, with the river continuing to flow on the Co. Down side, which was called Dargan Island in his honour.

A few years later 17 acres of Dargan Island was laid out as a pleasure garden and included a small zoo and a Crystal Palace, built of wood, iron and glass. According to Stephen Cameron in *Belfast Shipbuilders: A Titanic Tale*:

> 'Its centerpiece was a beautifully sculptured Italian fountain. On top of the fountain there was the figure of Neptune, with crown and trident, sitting on a large shell drawn by two fish horses, with water flowing from their mouths.'

Visitors were ferried across from the northern bank of the river and as well as the delights of the pleasure gardens the more adventurous could also go swimming. Belfast's Crystal Palace was destroyed by fire in 1864.

In 1843 the Ballast Board was replaced with the Belfast Harbour Commission who continued their contract with Dargan and on 10 July 1849 crowds gathered to witness the grand opening of the new Victoria Channel. The Commissioners and Dargan, on board the *Prince of Wales* and the regimental band of the 13th Irish Regiment, sailed down the channel past Dargan's Island (recently

---

8. The Ballast Board was set up in 1785 with 15 members including Samuel McTier who was the first Ballast Master. Its purpose was preserving and improving the Port and Harbour of Belfast.

The Men and Women who Built Belfast

renamed Queen's Island) where four cannons fired a salute. As the flotilla came to a stop Captain William Pirrie (grandfather of Lord Pirrie) made a short speech and then, depending on the source, poured either a bottle of Irish Whiskey or a bottle of Champagne into the river.

Queen Victoria had visited Belfast in August 1845 and it was to mark this visit that Dargan Island was renamed Queen's Island. When the Queen returned to Ireland in 1853 she visited Dargan at his home and offered him a knighthood, which he refused. In the same year he had helped to organize the Great Dubin Exhibition. Dargan's company helped to improve communications throughout the island of Ireland, from roads, to canals to railways. In 1866 he was seriously injured by being thrown by his horse and died a few months later in February 1867 in his Dublin home.

While the dredging and straightening of the river was intended to help with trade and industry, an unintended consequence was to provide the space on which Belfast's shipbuilding could thrive.

The Shipbuilders

The first ship that we know was built in Belfast was *Eagle Wing*. In 1636 local Presbyterians commissioned local carpenters and joiners to build a boat to take them and their congregations to a new life in America, free from what they saw as persecution[9] by the Church of Ireland. The ship left Belfast in September 1636 but in

---

9. Basically this was all part of the attempts by Charles I and the Anglican Church to exercise control over the church in Scotland/Presbyterians. The 39 Articles of Faith, which had been finalized in England in 1571, were approved in Ireland in 1634. John Bramwell, Archbishop of Armagh, supported Henry Leslie, the Bishop of Down & Connor, when he moved against five local Scottish ministers who would not accept this. He condemned them from a pulpit in Belfast, *'If he neglect to hear the church, let him be unto thee as an heathen man and a publican.'*

Famous Folk from Belfast

mid-Atlantic was badly damaged in a storm and limped back to Ireland, arriving at Groomsport on 3 November.[10]

For the next century and a half ship building in Belfast was rather haphazard, despite its growing shipping trade. Many ship owners would commission their vessels from other well-established ports, for example Captain John McCracken bought several boats in Liverpool. Then in 1791 a Scottish shipbuilder, William Ritchie, who had an established yard in Ayrshire, was invited over by the Ballast Board with the object to set up a shipyard in the town. He was attracted by the idea of a new venture with no competition and returned with his younger brother Hugh, ten skilled workmen and all the equipment that he needed. His first shipyard was a success and the first boat, *Hibernian*, was launched the following year. *Hibernian*, was built with an 'American bottom' which meant that merchants exporting goods could save 5% on customs duty.

Ritchie persuaded the Ballast Board to build the first dry dock in Belfast in 1800, No. 1 Clarendon Graving Dock, which is was at the back of the present day Harbour Commissioners Office. Before the dry dock was built his brother Hugh had set up his own shipyard further along the Lagan but he died in 1708 and another Ritchie brother, John, arrived from Scotland to take it over, renaming it John Ritchie and Sons.

Writing in 1811 William asserted:

> 'since the commencement [of the shipyard] I have built thirty-two vessels, and my brother eight, besides several lighters and small ones ... in my blacksmith shop all kinds of ship work are done in the best manner, also anchors of all sizes to 40 cwt.'

He employed around 130 men and had a weekly wage bill of £120 [£9,600]. The boats they built travelled around the world.

---

10. The annual Eagle Wing festival in Groomsport celebrates their safe return.

The Men and Women who Built Belfast

John Ritchie had set up a new partnership with another Scottish shipbuilder, Alexander McLaine, forming the Ritchie and McLaine yard. In 1820 William retired and his manager Charles Connell ran the business for him, before buying it in 1824 and changing the name to Charles Connell & sons. John Ritchie died in 1828 and McLaine took control of the company, changing the name to Alexander McLaine & sons. Another yard, McIlwaine and Lewis went through a similar series of name changes before becoming Workman Clark, the wee yard.

The Ritchie brothers had established the great shipbuilding tradition on the banks of the Lagan. The boats that they built were wooden, and they could source the material to build them on the island of Ireland, however innovations in the industry in the early nineteenth century could have sounded the death knell for the young shipyards, as many were driven by iron and coal, neither of which could be sourced in sufficient quantities close to home and had to be imported.

The same year as a sea captain's son was raising rebellion, Messrs McClenagh and Stainton established an iron foundry in Ballymacarrett, just outside the town boundaries. By 1802 both founders were dead and the new owner, Victor Coates had changed the name to Lagan Foundry. Before his retirement, William Ritchie had bought two 70 horsepower engines from the foundry for a new, wooden steamship, *Belfast*.

As with the shipyards, so a number of new foundries were established in Belfast including the Falls Foundry of Combe, Barbour and Combe, and Thomas Gladstone and Robert Pace's Ironworks in Eliza Street, which hoped to make boilerplates. They started production in the early 1850s but soon found that there was a major flaw in the their business plan. All their raw materials had to be imported and there wasn't a ready market for their product. In desperation they approached the Harbour Commissioners for

Famous Folk from Belfast

permission to open an iron shipyard on Queen's Island. A sub-committee chaired by Captain William Pirrie approved their application. Having gained the permission they cut their losses and sold the business to a Kerryman called Robert Hickson[11].

In 1853 Hickson leased a plot of land from the Harbour Commissioners on Queen's Island. It measured 100 x 500 feet and the lease included the provision of a slipway to be built by the Commissioners. The land was leased for 21 years and as the company grew so too did the amount of land it needed. When the company first opened on the site, in November 1853, the *Belfast News Letter* reported that:

> *'the business has been commenced in a spirit that augurs well for its future success and importance.'*

The confidence was not misplaced. A year later the company advertised for a new manager. The successful candidate was a twenty-three year old man called Edward James Harland.

Samuel Cleland Davidson

A few months ago I was watching a travel documentary starring Joanna Lumley. She was visiting a tea plantation in India and the owner of the plantation was explaining how they were able to pick and dry their own product, thus maximizing their profit. He pointed proudly at a large tea-drying machine, and there, embossed on the side was the legend *Sirocco, Belfast.*

The founder of the Sirocco works was Samuel Cleland Davidson, the son of James Davidson who owned flour mills in Belfast. Samuel was educated at Inst, but left at the age of 15 to take up an apprenticeship with William Hastings, a civil engineer. Samuel's uncle John owned a flax mill in Drumaness and was a pioneer in

---

11. Hickson went into partnership with James Spence to form Robert Hickson and Co.

the use of powered machinery to maximize profits. The nephew inherited the uncle's engineering curiosity.

When Samuel was eighteen his father and uncle bought a share in a tea plantation at Cachar in India and set up a tea importing company. The young Samuel was dispatched off to India to manage the plantation. It was here that his mechanical bent was able to develop. Away from parental control and removed from social activities he was able to experiment and eventually invented devices to mechanise almost every aspect of production.

It could be argued that he was actually assisted by both his remote location and lack of a formal university education. He was able to identify the problem and devise a solution, unaware that the current mechanical engineering theory dictated that it was impossible. It was a Heath Robinson approach and in later life he would often assert that, *'An ounce of fact is worth a ton of theory.'*

After a decade in India, and clutching his patented tea machinery blue-prints, he returned home to take up a position at the Combe, Barbour and Combe foundry to put his inventions into production. A couple of years later he was back in India with demonstration models of his tea-dryers. They proved to be so successful that they became [and as was demonstrated by Joanna Lumley] and remained the standard for the industry for decades.

In many ways Davidson can be compared to Lord Kelvin in that he used his own mechanical curiosity to devise patented solutions. For example his original tea-dryer led to him developing a highly efficient forward bladed centrifugal fan. His experiments also gave him the name for his company as it reminded someone who saw one of early prototype of the 'Sirocco' wind, and he adopted the name.

In 1881 the Sirocco Engineering works were opened in Belfast producing tea machinery, centrifugal supply and extractor fans. Their applications were not limited to the tea industry and his hot-air stoves, which remained cool to the touch, were rapidly adopted in the textile industry. His fans were used in ships in both the Royal and German navies and the merchant fleet, including the *Titanic*. During the First World War the company produced over 8,000 fans for the Royal and merchant navies. His ventilation system was adopted by the mining industry throughout the Empire and beyond. When the Royal Victoria Hospital was opened in 1903 it was equipped with the very latest Sirocco Air Conditioning system, supplied at cost.

The Sirocco works were unusual in that virtually everything they produced was an invention of Samuel's. His enquiring mind also saw him involved in experiments with rubber and even tennis net supports. His interest in the tea industry saw him opening the Sirocco Tea Store which brought the price of tea in Belfast down from 5 shillings to 2 shillings per pound.

Davidson was a Unionist in the Home Rule debates that dominated local politics during the late nineteenth century and early twentieth century, as he felt that Ireland in general and his company in particular would be better off within the economic union of the Empire, however when gangs threatened his Catholic employees and demanded that they were dismissed he refused and employed security guards to protect both them and the Works.

His eldest son and heir, James, was killed on the first day of the battle of the Somme and with his health failing he handed over management of the business to his son-in-law Frederick Maguire.

The Sirocco works site now stands derelict awaiting redevelopment but in parts of India the machines it once produced are still working.

The Men and Women who Built Belfast

The Workers of Belfast

In the space of one hundred and fifty years Belfast grew from a small town of 8,000 people to one of the most successful industrial cities in the world with a population of 386,947 in 1901. While the industrialists recorded above helped in that success, they could not have succeeded without the men, women and children who worked for them but whose names have been lost to time.

Too often the only time we learn their names is when their lives were in crisis, recorded in the court reports[12] or in the pages of the Belfast Charitable Societies Poorhouse or Hospital. But it is due to their hard work that Belfast prospered, often in horrific living and working conditions.

Writing in *Leviathan* in the seventeenth century Thomas Hobbes says that '*the life of man [is] solitary, poor, nasty, brutish, and short*'. This is a phrase that could easily be applied to the working class in Belfast for most of the eighteenth and nineteenth centuries. Writing in 1752 Lord Massereene said, '*I live in the neighbourhood of Belfast and know it to be in a ruinous condition*'. A century later it was a thriving industrial town with a population in 1851 of 87,000. Although in the second half of the nineteenth century the population growth was even more spectacular, the city fathers in the first hundred years of growth struggled to cope with the demands of a growing city.

The early industrialists and merchants were aware of both the dire conditions of the lower classes and their 'Christian' duty to try to help. It was this that drove the Joys et al to found the Belfast Charitable Society and build first the Poorhouse and then the infirmary, and future generations to found schools and campaign for

---

12. To hear some of their stories, or at least to learn their names, look up the excellent *Belfast Timeline*, which lists events and court proceedings from the 1830s onwards. It is free!

more hygienic working conditions as can be seen in a letter attributed to Mary Ann McCracken published in the *Belfast Newsletter* on the 17 May 1803 urging '*Proprietors of Cotton Mills, and other Factories*' to improve the working conditions by adhering to simple rules such as:

> '*The passages, stairs, floors and inner doors should be constantly kept clean, by sweeping, washing with soap and water … the walls whitewashed once a month … [as] The above operations appear best adapted for destroying effluvia or miasmate, the concomitant of all crowded rooms. Quicklime should daily be thrown into the houses of Convenience attached to large factories, which will effectively destroy all fetid effluvia … sufficient time should be allowed for amusement in the open air during fine weather, especially after the dinner hour.*'

The irony remained however that if a child found themselves an inmate of the Poorhouse they had a better chance of a good life than if they remained with their family in a poor district of the town. In the Poorhouse they were guaranteed a bed, clothing, food and a basic education. They were found apprenticeships and their apprentice masters were closely monitored to make sure they were properly trained and not abused. Contrast that to life outside the Poorhouse, where there were open drains and sewers, animals being slaughtered in the streets, recurrent food shortages caused by bad harvests and high prices, and unhygienic living and working conditions proved a breeding ground for malnutrition and disease. Even the most petty of crimes was punished severely. In October 1838 William Tully, a child of nine years, was sentenced to 12 months in jail with hard labour and whipped 3 times for stealing clothing. In the same year the Irish Poor Law Act introduced a system similar to that in England and removed responsibility from well-meaning organisations such as the Belfast Charitable Society to the more harshly regulated regime of the Workhouse, where admission depended upon total destitution.

The Men and Women who Built Belfast

As the century progressed and more and more people flooded into Belfast in search of employment, there were frequent cholera and typhus epidemics. In 1849 a Sanitary Committee was set up by Dr Andrew Malcolm to report into the conditions in the working-class districts, especially those with no proper drainage or sewerage and in 1852 he gave an address to the British Association that horrified its listeners. He asserted that due to the unusually high infant mortality rate, average life expectancy in Belfast was 9 years[13].

The large spinning mills brought employment to thousands but the work could also be dangerous. Drs C D and H S Purdon in the second half of the nineteenth century campaigned tirelessly to highlight the poor working conditions in the mills and the high accident rates. One particular disease that they highlighted was concentrated in the mill workers and was caused by the inhalation of flax dust. In his book *Longevity of Flax Mill and Factory Operatives (1875)* Purdon says that a girl who began in the Carding room aged 18 would probably be dead by the age of 30 because of this disease.

In the second half of the nineteenth century life did slowly begin to improve. Hundreds of new houses were built, a proper sewerage and drainage system was built and roads were properly laid out and paved. But areas of extreme poverty and insanitary housing remained as can be seen in the Hogg photographs held by the Ulster Museum and taken at the end of the century.

For those who had full employment the hours worked were very long, health and safety was almost non-existent and the workers had very few, if any rights. Employers imposed fines for the most petty of reasons such as laughing or talking, as well as more serious offences. The ability for workers to organize collectively was ham-

---

13. Some people try to say that the Great Famine distorted this figure, but his report was several years after the famine had ended and based on figures collated since 1849.

Famous Folk from Belfast

pered in Belfast by the growing sectarian divide that was utilized to good effect by those in whose interest it was to prevent that from happening.

However, the large textile mills provided employment for women as well as men, which meant that by the end of the nineteenth century the standard of living was higher in Belfast than in other industrial cities in Britain and the rest of Ireland.

While subject to downswings in the economy like every other industrial centre, employment figures were higher than elsewhere in Ireland. A series of employment regulations removed young children from the workforce and provided them with a basic education, something the Joy family had been trying to achieve in the 1780s. Workers had more leisure time and late nineteenth and early twentieth century Belfast had Variety Theatres, bars, lending libraries, night classes, churches, and public parks to cater to every taste.

The next time you walk through the streets of Belfast, or along the banks of the Lagan, pause and think about the people who physically built Belfast.

It is no mean city and they were no mean people.

Belfast and its Forgotten History

Belfast was not meant to be a major city. In fact for most of its existence it was very much in the shadow of Carrickfergus, a few miles along the Co. Antrim coast. While there is evidence of human habitation in Belfast dating back to Neolithic times, what we think of as Belfast is only a couple of hundred years old. For most of its existence it was a strategic crossing point of the river Lagan, but that was about it. There were a series of wooden and later stone forts or castles built to defend the crossing, and the fact that they were burnt to the ground on a regular basis is a good indication of how important control of the area was, but the real power was invested, at least from the arrival of the Anglo-Normans onwards, in the castle at Carrickfergus.

The seventeenth century was tumultuous for much of Ireland and Britain with the civil war, execution of Charles I, the Commonwealth, the Restoration in 1660, the 'Glorious Revolution' of 1688 and the subsequent Williamite wars in Ireland. However, despite the fact that various opposing armies occupied the town, Belfast was not only left untouched but also its merchants and publicans actually managed to profit from the influx of soldiers and its position at the mouth of the Lagan saw it develop both as a market town and an increasingly important port.

Despite its relatively untroubled gestation, as a mere youth compared to Dublin, Edinburgh or London, in the intervening years Belfast has exhibited many of the traits of teenager – rapid growth, boundless energy, radical views, mood swings and tantrums making its history a rich tapestry indeed.

Famous Folk from Belfast

We all think that we know Belfast's history, but little history arrives with us fully intact as various forces over the intervening years have conspired to manipulate it for their own ends. Some would claim that alternative facts and fake news are a recent phenomena but in truth they have always been with us.

In Belfast this is especially so with two competing traditions emerging in the latter part of the 19th century seeking to bend history to fit their own narrative. This has resulted in one side or the other glossing over certain aspects or, in cases where it suits neither side's narrative, being forgotten completely.

Take James Magennis VC as an example. The Unionist establishment was embarrassed because Northern Ireland's only VC in the second world war was a working class catholic and the Nationalist establishment was embarrassed because Northern Ireland's only VC in the second world war was a working class catholic so he was quietly forgotten.

The following are three examples of where events have to some extent been swept under the carpet as they don't quite fit with a popular narrative.

The Belfast Volunteers.

Most people will have heard about the United Irishmen, the summer soldiers, whose failed rebellion in 1798 was a major contributing factor to the subsequent Act of Union in 1800. However, they were heavily influenced by the earlier Belfast Volunteers, and in many cases had actually been Volunteers. So to understand the United Irishmen it is important to first examine the Volunteers.

To set the scene we must first look at a couple of circumstances and events. Although Ireland had her own parliament it was subservient to that in Westminster. Since the turn of the century the English parliament had enacted a series of measures which placed

Forgotten History

substantial tariffs on goods being imported from Ireland, while forbidding the Irish parliament to do the same. The result was that the Irish woollen, silk and glass industries were almost destroyed. Linen only survived because the land and climate in Ireland was better suited to growing flax, but even it was only domestic in nature. Added to this was the fact that the country suffered from frequent bad harvests and localised famines.

The result was that in the years immediately preceding the outbreak of the American War of Independence, thousands of young men and women had left the island, but especially the northern counties to travel in search of a better life in the American colonies. A report in the *Belfast NewsLetter* in 1773 stated that in the previous two years over 17,000 had emigrated and that *'the North of Ireland has in the five or six years been drained of one fourth of its trading cash and the like proportion of the manufacturing people.'* The revolutionary colonists were, therefore, the sons, daughters, uncles, aunts, brothers and sisters of the people in Belfast.

The enthusiasm for the American revolt was tempered by the arrival, in April 1778, of an American privateer, Paul Jones, in Belfast Lough and then almost totally dissipated by France joining the side of the rebels. No matter how sympathetic they may be to their kinsmen across the water, they hated and feared the French, *'the jealous enemies of our liberties and religion'*. Many had good reason to do so as they were descendants of French Huguenots who had escaped religious persecution in France just a few decades earlier.

As the war in America had continued the island of Ireland had been left almost defenceless in the face of a feared invasion as troops were sent out of the country. So when their appeal to the Lord Lieutenant went unanswered the burgesses and merchants of Belfast, as Lord Charlemont wrote,

Famous Folk from Belfast

> *'Abandoned by the Government in the hour of Danger, the inhabitants of Belfast were left to their own defense and boldly and instantly undertook it.'*

The Belfast Volunteers were formed on St Patrick's Day and recruitment was swift. By June they held their first church parade in scarlet and black uniforms, of Irish Manufacture. As rumours of an imminent French invasion spread so more and more Volunteer militia were formed, especially as it was apparent that the Irish administration lacked the ability to defend the island.

The men who had joined the ranks of the Volunteers were steeped in the radical theories of political thought that had been put forward by the figures of the Enlightenment in Scotland and throughout Europe. The Volunteers were run on the latest democratic system. Officers were elected and, in Belfast, their numbers included Presbyterians and even a few Catholic merchants. As the threat of invasion faded the drills gave way to debate and the main topic of conversation was political reform. This culminated on 15 February 1781 at the Dungannon Convention where they passed the motion that:

> *'In a free country the voice of the People must prevail. We know our duty to our Sovereign, and are loyal. We know our duty to ourselves, and are resolved to be Free. We seek for our Rights and no more than our Rights.'*

While it would be nice to think that the parliament that was elected in the wake of this declaration, [better known as Grattan's Parliament, as it was dominated by the Patriot Party], was able to deliver on all the aspiration for a free and democratic society, it wasn't. Nor were the demands for catholic emancipation accepted. However, while in the rest of the country the Volunteer movement declined after the end of the war in America, in Belfast it stayed as strong, and as radical as ever, celebrating the news of the French revolution with bonfires and marking the anniversary of the fall of

Forgotten History

the Bastille with a parade and celebrations. It was at one such celebration in 1791 that the Society of United Irishmen was formed.

The Volunteer movement and its aspirations ultimately ended in failure and the Belfast Volunteers, who campaigned for Catholic Emancipation were not remembered even though distorted echoes of the movement were felt long after. It was the first time that a paramilitary force had attempted to influence the politics of the nation. It was not just a coincidence that opponents and supporters of Home Rule over a century later formed themselves into Volunteer forces.

The Famine

For our next example of forgotten history we must fast forward into the 1840s. The Act of Union had been passed, the Royal Academical Institution was opened in 1810, the first hospital was opened in 1815, Daniel O'Connell had succeeded in achieving Catholic emancipation in 1829 the same year that a lunatic asylum was opened in Belfast, the Ulster Museum was founded the next year, the Botanic gardens and palm house were opened in 1840 and in 1845 the Queen's College opened its doors to male students. The population of Belfast had grown from around 20,000 in 1800 to 70,000 in 1841 as people flooded in from the countryside to find employment in the mills, factories, foundries and shipyards. In many cases they were driven off the land by short leases, rising rents, and frequent bad harvests resulting in famine[1]. These additional 50,000 were crowded into the old town that was recorded as being an area of one and a half square miles. Despite the efforts of the Corporation, the Belfast Charitable Society and

---

1. Patrick Fitzgerald in *'Great Hunger? Irish Famine: Changing patterns of crisis'* The Hungry Stream – essays on emigration and famine ed Margaret Crawford, outlines four failures of the harvest and potato crop in the twenty-five years before 1845.

the newly opened Workhouse [1841] this was a breeding ground for disease. Then in 1845 the potato harvest failed.

Anyone who has taken no more than a passing interest in the Great Famine would be forgiven for thinking that it only effected the southern counties of Ireland and then only the rural catholic population. Some commentators have gone so far as to suggest that it was an attempt at genocide by an uncaring vindictive government. The truth as always is not so simple. As Christine Kinealy and Gerard MacAtasney state in *The Hidden Famine [2000]*,

> '*the traditional orthodoxy has been that the Famine had little impact on the northeastern corner of Ireland, especially on the Protestant population. Contemporary evidence suggests otherwise.*'

Belfast and its hinterland was predominantly Protestant, the Catholic population in the years immediately before the Famine was only around 20% and areas of Belfast such as Ballymacarrett were almost 100% Protestant. Most of the farmers were able to supplement their incomes with various aspects of the linen industry, but this meant that the amount of land they could devote to food crops was decreased, which led to a dependence on the potato crop. The problem with the act of genocide argument is that an organic viral fungus is unable to distinguish between a 'protestant' field of potatoes and a 'catholic' field as the blight spread throughout the island in the summer of 1845 and reports about it started to appear in the *Belfast Newsletter* and the *Banner of Ulster* newspapers.

One way to think about the Famine in relation to Belfast is that it was a perfect storm. While it was an industrial town, the abundance of labour kept wages low and houses overcrowded. There was a recently opened Workhouse, capable of housing 1,000, but the Belfast Guardians who administered it had been reluctant to include the highly industrialised area of Ballymacarrett into the union, as it lay on the other side of the Lagan. In addition there was an economic downturn in both the linen and cotton industry, which was outside their control, but as we shall see had disastrous results for the cotton workers in Ballymacarrett.

When the blight returned the following year, accompanied by a poor harvest of other crops such as carrots, oats and turnips, what had started off as a trickle into the town in search of food, employment or a ship's passage the Belfast Union was overwhelmed. Between 1841 and 1851 the population had grown from 75,308 to 100,301. When it was all over and the powers that be decided to forget it was often stated that the Belfast Union was one of the few in the country not to apply for government loans for assistance in famine relief but they did this by relying on privately funded relief, such as soup kitchens run by, you guessed it, Mary Ann McCracken et al. Meanwhile in Holywood farmers were dumping the blighted potatoes into the sea and disease was finding a fertile breeding ground amongst the crowded hovels in the city and emaciated population. By the end of 1846 the distress in Ballymacarrett was being likened to the distress in Skibbereen.

Even before the famine Ballymacarrett had been in dire straits. It was a centre of the cotton industry but Scottish companies owned most of the mills and so when there was a severe economic depression in Glasgow, the weavers of Belfast had their wages cut to a pittance or were made unemployed, around 600 in total. The changes in the Poor Law meant that they could only be admitted to the workhouse when they had lost everything and the *Belfast Newsletter*'s editorial railed

> '*Is not the insufficiency of the Poor Law system clearly seen, when so much distress prevails throughout the country and it can do nothing to relieve it?*'

In March 1846 the *Banner of Ulster* reported that many of the people of Ballymacarrett were subsisting on one meal a day and were

Famous Folk from Belfast

'in absolute danger of starvation, perhaps before another week, unless effective relief be procured.'

Nor was Ballymacarrett the only district badly effected. In March 1847 the Belfast Ladies' Clothing Society[2] had provided blankets and clothes to over 1,000 families in Ballyhackamore, Ballynafeigh and Ballymacarrett and opened an industrial training school for young girls, which provided board and lodgings. As emaciated men, women and children succumbed to disease in 1847 the Poor Law Guardians had to purchase three acres at Blackstaff New Road to provide new graves. At a town meeting the same year the Rev Richard Oltan described the situation at the Shankill graveyard:

'Coffins are heaped upon coffins until the last one is often not more than two inches underground and in finding room for others, bodies that have not been long buried are often exhumed.'

The town authorities were overwhelmed and seemed to be unable to comprehend the scale of the tragedy unfolding in front of their eyes. Public meetings attended by the usual suspects such as Andrew Mulholland and William Sharman Crawford urged measures such as the suspension of distillation, so that the cereal could be used to feed the poor, as had happened earlier in the century, but this was outside the control of the authorities. However, not everyone was so sympathetic to their plight and in a reflection of the *Laissez Faire* school of political thought then prevalent the *Northern Whig* opposed the idea of appealing for government assistance:

'We almost dread that in a short time we shall see even the people of Belfast degrading themselves by going before the government to implore some crumbs of charity ... we shall have to witness the humiliation of external alms among ourselves.'

---

2. Go on; guess who was a founding member!

Forgotten History

In 1847 the Belfast Orange Order ordered that no music was to be played at their July commemoration in recognition of the calamity that had:

> *'thinned out our local population and removed many of our Loyal brethren.'*

So why have we forgotten to remember the famine in Belfast? I think there is a hint in the excerpt from the *Northern Whig*. There was a sense of shame that Belfast, who saw itself as so much more successful than other cities was unable to cope. It didn't apply for government help, so in later decades could fool itself that it hadn't needed it or if it was remembered it was something that had only happened to the in-comers, not the long term residents, a tragedy – yes – but nothing really to do with us. But yet the evidence of the unfolding disaster is still visible in the pages of the newspapers of the day. The first Home Rule bill was presented around thirty years later, when many of those who had lived through the events were still alive. However the 'story' had moved on. It didn't suit those who were opposed to Home Rule to remember the suffering. That didn't fit the narrative, and those in favour of Home Rule didn't want to remember that the Great Famine had been a national tragedy in Ireland, that it had effected every denomination. The Great Famine resulted in the poorest in society dying in the streets of Belfast from hunger and disease. It should be remembered by everyone.

Women's Emancipation

As the horrors of the famine faded and those that died were only dimly remembered by the survivors, Belfast settled down to becoming the leading industrial town in Ireland, with occasional bouts of sectarian rioting to relieve the boredom and keep everyone in their proper place.

Famous Folk from Belfast

Unusually the workforce included a high proportion of women, needed to keep the linen mills working at full capacity. This resulted in a higher standard of living for the women and their children. It was the fact that these wages were deemed to be the property of their husbands that prompted Isabella Tod to take up an invitation to appear before the committee of MPs researching the Married Woman's Property Bill in 1868. In reply to a question from the MPs she stated:

> *"I know a number of cases in which the women are hardly able to maintain themselves and their families at all, because their husbands take their wages from them, or a very considerable proportion of them when they receive them, more frequently perhaps they run up debts at the public houses which the women must discharge at least under threat of having their furniture or other property taken to pay for it, and the consequences are very bad for all the family."*

As early as 1796 Mary Ann McCracken had written to Harry as he languished in Kilmainham:

> *'Is it not almost time for the clouds of error and prejudice to disperse and that the female parts of the Creation as well as the male should throw off the fetters with which they have so long mentally bound and conscious of the dignity and importance of their nature rise to the situation for which they were designed ... there can be no argument produced in favour of the slavery of woman that has not been used in favour of general slavery.'*

And while she was unable to persuade the United Irishmen to include female emancipation along with catholic in their aims, the rest of her life was spent trying to provide the young girls in the Poorhouse with an education and training that would help them become independent. The irony was that the middle-class early Victorian granddaughters of her classmates at David Manson's school had a far more restrictive education than she had received herself and in many cases it was of a poorer standard than the girls in her care.

This did not mean that there was no appetite for change. Mary Ann was still alive and active in charitable organisations in 1859 when the 27-year-old Margaret Byers opened an 'Establishment for the Boarding and Education of Young Ladies'[3] at 15 Wellington Place. There is no evidence that either Margaret Byers or her good friend Isabella Tod ever met Mary Ann, but I think that it is probable as they were involved in many of the same causes and moved in similar social circles. I like to think of them sitting beside the old lady, listening to her tales of old Belfast and taking inspiration from her activism.

A couple of years after Mary Ann's death Isabella and Margaret founded the North of Ireland Women's Suffrage Committee, the first such organisation in Ireland. Both were informed by their membership of the Presbyterian Church. As full congregant members they were allowed to vote to elect committeemen, elders and the congregation's minister. So why were they not allowed to vote for their MP? Both women were able to use their considerable contacts to try to change life for women in Ireland. Margaret is best known for her success in opening up full and equal education to girls, up to and including university degrees, even travelling over to London with Isabella in 1878 to lobby in the heart of government to have girls included in the new Intermediate Education (Ireland) Act, which provided for standardized examinations throughout all ages of school children.

Isabella did have some local success in her search for female suffrage. In the 1880s the Belfast Corporation at last turned its attention to the vexed question of adequate sewerage and drainage. The resulting scheme meant a rise in the local rate and for the first

---

3. This was to evolve into Victoria College.

time all ratepayers were given the vote in local elections. Isabella persuaded Lord Erne to move an amendment to the local franchise bill in the House of Lords to change the word 'man' to 'person' with an explanatory clause showing that the word 'person' meant man or woman.

She travelled tirelessly gathering support for her assertion that:

> *'the possession of the franchise ... is an absolute necessity. It is impossible for women to do their duty and to protect their interests and dignity without the same weapon men find essential for the same purposes.'*

The two women were suffragists, but other women in Belfast including Winifred Carney were attracted to Mrs Pankhurst's more militant suffragette movement the Women's Social and Political Union and flocked to listen to her speak at the Ulster Hall. I like to think that had she still been alive Mary Ann would have been in the front row. Harry Ferguson's aunt, the redoubtable Dr Elizabeth Gould Bell was there and was imprisoned in London for her suffragette activities. She was also actively involved in the arson attacks and acts of vandalism that took place in and around Belfast.

I have searched in vain for mention of a movement that concerned over half the population of Belfast in some of the more recognised histories of the city. Should it be mentioned at all it is confined to at best one or two sentences, and yet it embraced all strata of society and both communities. So why the silence?

The answer has to be Home Rule.

Home Rule split the Irish women's suffrage movement the same as the rest of society. Unsurprisingly many of the leaders in the north, such as Isabella Tod, were opposed to it. In Tod's case it was because she felt that women's issues were better protected within the wider political union with Britain, due to the conservative forces rife in Irish life, namely the churches. She was a Liberal Unionist

Forgotten History

and in 1886 formed the Liberal Women's Unionist Association in Belfast. This lost her many close friends within the movement both in Ireland and in England, and this is probably the main reason why she remains relatively unknown today. Within the anti-Home Rule movement, Sir Edward Carson[4] promised full female emancipation only to back down later. This betrayal aroused the fury of many more militant suffragettes, such as Dr Bell, and within six months thirteen suffragettes were imprisoned for arson attacks on Unionist leaders houses and property. On the pro-Home Rule side, suffragists such as Winifred Carney and Alice Milligan found themselves being drawn down a more radical route.

Belfast had a history of over one hundred years of struggle for women's suffrage, an unbroken line from Mary Ann McCracken to Winifred Carney and Margaret McCoubrey. Why we do not have streets named after the women who fought so long and so hard for equal rights? Why they have been written out of history.

Too often in our society with its divided education system we are only exposed to one version of history. When I think about the forgotten history, I am reminded of the late Tony Benn M.P. He was a great defender of radical politics and democracy, in fact he would probably have felt very much at home in the Belfast of 1791. He said that you should always ask anybody in a position of power five questions. One of which was *In whose interests do you use it?* The same principles can be applied to the forgotten history. Why is our shared history not known? In whose interest is it that we have forgotten our shared history?

---

4. In September 1913 a letter was published that said that plans were being drawn up for a provisional government that would include female franchise.

Dear Reader,

I hope you have enjoyed this publication from Ballyhay Books, an imprint of Laurel Cottage Ltd. We publish an eclectic mix of books ranging from personal memoirs to authoritative books on local history, from sport to poultry, from photographs to fiction and from music to marine interests – but all with a distinctly local flavour.

To see details of these books, as well as the beautifully illustrated books of our sister imprint Cottage Publications, why not visit our website **www.cottage-publications.com** or telephone +44 (0)28 9188 8033.

Timothy S Johnston

BALLYHAY BOOKS